The Havanese

By Diane Klumb

With Joanne Baldwin DVM

Photos by Joanne Baldwin DVM (unless otherwise credited)

Special thanks to Richi Shinn for invaluable technical assistance in preparing this manuscript for publication.

This Book is dedicated to . . .

. . . Diego who, despite being born of health-tested
parents and nurtured by a conscientious breeder,
died at five weeks of age, weighing only one pound.
RNA submitted from Diego and other dogs belonging
to dedicated Havanese fanciers will, one day, help us
solve the mystery and heartbreak of Ockham Syndrome so that future Diegos grow happy and healthy.
It is for Diego and with the goal of solving Havanese
health issues that the proceeds from this book will be
donated to H.E.A.R.T. for the TAMU Havanese Genetics Project until the grant total is reached.

THE HAVANESE

CONTENTS

30. Petit Chien havane.

The look of the Havanese was well established by 1856
—Photo from HCA Archives

Chapter 1

THE HAVANESE...

Its History and Character

Like a troupe of little Rumba dancers, the Havanese burst upon the American show scene in 1999, all ruffles and charm, a virtual unknown in the world of dogs. Soaring in popularity, they seemed to have emerged from nowhere, leading many to believe that the Havanese is a new breed, perhaps a recent cross.

*Amazingly, the breed developed over the past three centuries a **mere ninety miles** from America's shore. It's often called the world's longest ninety miles, that stretch of azure water known as the Florida Straits... for this is the National Dog of Cuba.*

Christopher Columbus called Cuba the "Pearl of the Antilles"

A Dog of Many Names.......

The Havanese is considered to be Cuba's only native breed, and there is ample written historical evidence that it was, indeed, developed there sometime prior to the seventeenth century, but it is not indigenous to the island. Recent developments in canine genomic research reveal that few if any domestic dogs are actually indigenous - the country of origin is simply where a breed was developed. Each breed, to a great degree, reflects both its function and the character of the people who created it, and the Havanese is no exception. Developed on a small tropical island purely as a companion animal, the unique coat, ideal for the island's climate, and the undeniably Latin personality both mirror its Cuban roots to perfection.

Theories about the origins of the Havanese abound, many of them with little or no historical basis. Many 19th century dog writers simply postulated, with little or no research or even historical logic, that they were the result of various crosses, the most widespread story being a cross between an early Cuban dog and the "Argentinean Poodle". Aside from this single reference, there appears to be no trace of such a dog ever *existing* in Argentina at any point in time. Likewise, tales of 19th Century Italian sea captains bringing them to Cuba are also entirely without basis, as the breed was already established, and written about, by 1700!

The *real* problem one encounters when researching the history of the Havanese is that the breed has had so many different *names* over the centuries - the Blanquito de la Cubano, or White Cuban, in the early 1700s; the Dog of Havannah (in the late 1700s); the Cuban Shock-dog (so-called for the familiar shock of hair that falls over his eyes), the Cuba-dog, and the Havana Spaniel (all in the 1800s); le Havanais (in France around the turn of the century); and, of course, the one that appears in several references over the years and has the advantage of being wonderfully descriptive - the Havana Silk Dog.

The name Havanese (originally Toy Havanese), in fact, appears to have been coined in the United States, sometime in the early 1970s, and the average Cuban who left the island prior to the revolution has never heard of one - until recently, the Cubans have called them Maltese!

What has *never* changed over the past three centuries is the recurring description of a small, silky-coated dog from Cuba which came in a myriad of colors and, according to one 19th Century writer, which often had cords that dragged upon the floor. A rose, as we know, by any other name would smell as sweet and the same is true of our little dogs from Cuba. What follows is a fairly *accurate* history of the breed, pieced together from extensive research of historical documents.

The island of Cuba was settled shortly after its discovery, by Columbus near the end of the fifteenth century, by two distinct groups, which formed the basis for Cuba's future class culture. The first (and most important if one wished to carve a civilization out of wilderness) were farmers, laborers, and craftsmen from the Spanish-owned Canary Islands, including the island of Tenerife, who were granted *peonias,* or small tracts of land. The second were the *segundones*, or "second sons" of the Spanish aristocracy who, unable to inherit land and title in Spain, often set off for the colonies, holding land grants for substantial *caballerias*, to make their fortunes.

Since earliest times, dogs have accompanied man on his journeys to new worlds and the settling of Cuba was no exception. Ship's logs of the early 16th century voyages record dogs on board, along with the settlers, and it is not unlikely that some of these were the small dogs of Tenerife, generally recognized as the common ancestors of the Bichon family of dogs. As Spain imposed fairly draconian trade restrictions on its Caribbean colonies, and the port of Tenerife was one of the few open to Cuba for trade, it is highly likely that the dogs developed with little outside influence.

By the early 1700s, these dogs apparently found their way into the homes of the Cuban landed gentry, the *caballeros*, were much admired and accompanied their owners on extended vacations to Europe. Often white, or mostly so, these dogs were referred to by European dog writers of the time as the Blanquito de la Cubano (the White Cuban) , the Dog of Havannah, or the Havana Silk Dog.

Charming, beribboned and pampered, they found entry through their socially well-connected owners into the courts of England, Spain and France where, in the latter two countries, they were often shorn in the manner of the larger European Poodle. As early as 1700, Britain's Queen Anne, much taken with the breed after seeing a troupe of them perform at Court, obtained two for herself and appears to be the earliest Havanese owner of note.

She was followed in the next century by the noted canine aficionado HRH Queen Victoria, whose pair of "Cuba dogs", (Chico and Golia, by name) was obtained for her directly from Havana by a Lady Ellesmere. They were apparently also popular among Britain's literati and, as these fellows were notoriously verbose, quite a bit was written about the life and times of these small Cuban charmers in the nineteenth century. Both Charles Dickens and his close friend, the philosopher Thomas Carlyle, wrote extensively about their little Cuban "Shock-dogs", named Timmy and Nero, respectively. (Nero, in fact, lies buried to this day in Thomas Carlyle's garden.)

The fortunes of the Havanese have always risen and fallen with the politics of the times. Popular among the aristocracy of both Cuba and Europe until the early part of the twentieth century, little is recorded of the breed in the next fifty years. Two World Wars in Europe created sweeping social change and no record exists of the descendants of the little dogs from Havana who found their way to the courts of England, Spain, and France. None are believed to have survived the chaos of the ensuing decades. That they existed there at all is only evidenced through the examination of dog shows records from the early 1900s, and by the fact that written Standards for the breed date from that period.

The little dogs fared no better in their homeland. As Cuba's "sugar barons" sold out to large American firms, and its ruling class was replaced by a strong bourgeoisie, the Havanese, or "Maltese" as they were called there, adapted, becoming family pets of this new class of professionals, watching over both the children and the ubiquitous small family poultry flocks that were kept for eggs in suburban Havana, but the breed was not particularly popular in Cuba during most of the twentieth century, and was largely ignored by the rest of the world.

The Modern Havanese

The Cuban Revolution changed the fortunes of the little Havanese once again. The class of Cubans most likely to own them was, not surprisingly, among the first to leave. A small number of dogs found their way to both Costa Rica and the US with their expatriate owners after the revolution and, in 1979, the Havanese Club of America, now the AKC Parent Club for the breed, was formed. Beginning with the pedigrees of 9 breeding age dogs (8 of whose descendants formed the foundation of the AKC Stud book) from two different bloodlines assembled by the club's first president, Mrs. Dorothy Goodale of Colorado, the first registry for Havanese in the breed's history was created. Early dogs from this registry were exported to Western Europe in the early 80s, where they have achieved a fair measure of popularity at FCI shows. The descendents of these 8 dogs make up the larger percentage of the gene pool of the Havanese breed today, now estimated to be over 8,000 in number.

This original gene pool has been expanded in the last decade worldwide by the addition of Havanese from Russia and Hungary. These dogs are believed to have accompanied their comrades home from extended government embassy appointments, and cultural exchange programs during the 70s and 80s, when the Soviet Bloc maintained a strong physical presence in the Castro regime. Although the breed was never registered with the stud book there (or even in Cuba *prior* to its arrival in the Soviet Union) it was accepted into the Hungarian Stud Book sometime prior to 1990. (It is interesting to note that the Havanese was registered in Hungary as a Toy breed with full privileges *ten years* before they were accepted into the AKC Toy Group!) Once registered in Hungary, these

Russian dogs were quickly crossed with dogs from Holland and Germany originally obtained from the small US gene pool, and so there is no "pure Russian blood" left there today. Hungarian-bred dogs of any AKC breed with MET registration are eligible for AKC registration, as the AKC has accepted the Hungarian stud book for many decades. On the other hand, it is important to know that many Russian-bred Havanese being imported in recent years (mostly by pet shops and dog brokers) are *not* eligible for AKC registration, nor are their offspring.

More recently a few dogs have been exported to Western Europe and Canada directly from Cuba, where a small number remained after the revolution. An effort has been made there to reestablish the country's only native breed, and in 1993, the Havanese, (or Bichon Habanero, as it is now called in its native land), was officially designated the National Dog of Cuba, and accepted into the Cuban Stud Book, ironically for the first time in its 300 year history. Dogs bred in Cuba are ineligible for AKC registration at this time. Potential buyers of all imported Havanese, *or their offspring*, would be wise to contact the AKC's Foreign Registration Dept. *before* purchase, as rules vary from country to country.

The Havanese Club of America maintained its own stud book from 1979 until Dec. 1,1995, when the Havanese became a member of the AKC Miscellaneous Group in its first step toward full American Kennel Club recognition. (It is interesting to note that all the dogs entered in the HCA studbook at the time it was turned over to AKC were designated as *foundation stock*, and this notation is still sometimes seen in older pedigrees.) The Havanese Club of America awarded its own HCA Championships from 1984 until January 1999, when the Havanese joined the Toy Group and was granted full AKC championship privileges.

The first HCA Standard for the breed was written in 1981, and expanded upon the earlier FCI Standard from Europe, which had existed in some form from the early days of the twentieth century, when dogs exported from Cuba were exhibited at shows there. This first Standard essentially described the dogs that comprised the original breeding stock; it depicted the ideal Havanese as slightly longer than tall, with an almond eye, a springy gait, and a rise in the topline, not more than 10½ inches tall and weighing not more than 13½ lbs.

The Standard was revised several times over the years and, after recognition by AKC, was revised again, in an effort to both return it to its original intent and to comply with the standardized formatting desired by the American Kennel Club. This Standard, in use today, was approved by the HCA membership in November of 2000 and by AKC for its use on June 21, 2001. It describes the "ideal" Havanese from nose to tail, and provides a clear blueprint for the breed.

On January 1, 1999, the Havanese joined the AKC Toy Group and its popularity has soared since then as more Americans discover the charms of this little Cuban ragmop. The Havanese Club of America, now the licensed AKC Parent Club for the breed, is dedicated to preserving, responsibly promoting, and protecting the interests of the Havanese at the National

---

Famous Havanese Owners of the Past

HRH Queen Anne of England
HRH Queen Victoria of England
Charles Dickens, author
Thomas Carlyle, philosopher
Earnest Hemingway, author

level. The Club sponsors both local and National AKC Specialty shows, where progress made by breeders in both breed type and soundness are measured, as well as AKC performance events. In addition, the Club supports educational programs for the public, breeders, and judges, supports health research in the breed, maintains a Placement Assistance and Rescue Committee for Havanese in need of new homes, and maintains a Cuban Relief Committee, which buys and sends vaccines and other needed supplies to its sister club in Cuba. The HCA maintains an informational website at www.havanese.org.

The AKC Havanese Standard

Standards for many breeds, especially those written many years ago, are notoriously brief, and lend themselves easily to subjective interpretation. The current AKC Havanese Standard does not fall into this category - quite famously long, it covers every conceivable part of the dog. It is presented here in its entirety.

General Appearance: The Havanese is a small sturdy dog of immense charm. He is slightly longer than tall, and covered with a profuse mantle of untrimmed long, silky, wavy hair. His plumed tail is carried loosely curled over his rump. A native of Cuba, he has evolved over the centuries from the pampered lapdog of the aristocracy into what he is today - the quintessential family pet of a people living on a small tropical island. His duties traditionally have been those of companion, watchdog, child's playmate and herder of the family poultry flock. His presentation in the show ring should reflect his function - always in excellent condition but never so elaborately coifed as to preclude an impromptu romp in the leaves, as his character is essentially playful rather than decorative.

While historically always a toy dog and therefore never overly large or coarse, he does not appear so fragile as to make him unsuitable as a child's pet. His unique coat reflects centuries in the tropics, and protects against the heat. It is remarkably soft and light in texture, profuse without being harsh or woolly. Likewise, the furnishings of the head are believed to protect the eyes from the harsh tropical sun, and have traditionally never been gathered in a topknot for this reason.

In both structure and gait, the Havanese is not easily mistaken for any other breed. His characteristic topline, rising slightly from withers to rump is a result of moderate angulation both fore and aft combined with a typically short upper arm. The resulting springy gait is flashy rather than far-reaching and unique to the breed. The overall impression of the dog on the move is

18

one of agility rather than excessive ability to cover ground. These characteristics of temperament, structure and gait contribute in large part to the character of the breed, and are essential to type.

Size, Proportion, and Substance: The height range is from 8 1/2 to 11 1/2 inches, with the ideal being between 9 and 10 1/2 inches, measured at the withers, and is slightly less than the length from point of shoulder to point of buttocks, creating a rectangular outline rather than a square one. The Havanese is a sturdy little dog, and should never appear fragile. A coarse dog with excessive bone is likewise contrary to type and therefore equally undesirable. The minimum height ranges set forth in the description above shall not apply to dogs or bitches under twelve months of age.

Disqualification: Height at withers under 8 1/2 inches or over 11 1/2 inches, except that the minimum height ranges set forth in the description above shall not apply to dogs or bitches under twelve months of age.

Head: The expression is soft and intelligent, mischievous rather than cute. The eyes are dark brown, large, almond-shaped, and set rather widely apart. Dark eyes are preferred irrespective of coat color, although the chocolate colored dog may have somewhat lighter eyes. The pigment on the eyerims is complete, solid black for all colors except for the chocolate dog which has complete solid, dark chocolate brown pigment. No other dilution of pigment is acceptable. Ears are of medium length; the leather, when extended, reaches halfway to the nose. They are set high on the skull, slightly above the endpoint of the zygomatic arch, and are broad at the base, showing a distinct fold. When the dog is alert, the ears lift at the base, producing an unbroken shallow arc from the outer edge of each ear across the backskull. The backskull is broad and slightly rounded. The stop is moderate. Length of muzzle is slightly less than length of backskull measured from stop to point of occiput and the planes are level. The nose is broad and squarish, fitting a full and rectangular muzzle, with no indication of snipiness. The pigment on the nose and lips is complete, solid black for all colors except for the chocolate dog which has complete solid, dark chocolate brown pigment. No other dilution of pigment is acceptable. A scissors bite is ideal. Full complement of incisors preferred.

Disqualifications: Complete absence of black (or chocolate in the chocolate dog) pigmentation on the eyerims, nose or lips

Neck, Topline and Body: The neck is of moderate length, in balance with the height and length of the dog. It carries a slight arch and blends smoothly into the shoulders. The topline is straight but not level, rising slightly from withers to rump. There is no indication of a roach back. The body, measured from point of shoulder to point of buttocks, is slightly longer than the height at the withers. This length comes from the ribcage and not from the short, well-muscled loin. The chest is deep, rather broad in front, and reaches the elbow. The ribs are well sprung. There is a moderate tuck-up. The tail is high-set and plumed with long, silky hair. It arcs forward over the back, but neither lies flat on the back nor is tightly curled. On the move the tail is carried loosely curled over the rump. The long plume of hair may fall straight forward or to either side of the body. The tail may not be docked.

Forequarters: Shoulder layback is moderate, lying not more than 40 degrees off vertical. Extreme shoulder layback will negatively affect proper gait, and should be faulted. The tops of the shoulder blades lie in at the withers, allowing the neck to merge smoothly into the back. The upper arm is relatively short, but there is sufficient angle between the shoulder and upper arm to set the legs well under the body with a pronounced forechest. The elbows turn neither in nor out, and are tight to the body. Forelegs are well boned and straight when viewed from any angle. The distance from the foot to the elbow is equal to the distance from elbow to withers. The pasterns are short, strong and flexible, very slightly sloping. Dewclaws may be removed. The feet are round, with well-arched toes, and turn neither in nor out. Pads and nails may be black, white, pink or a combination of these colors. Chocolate dogs may also have brown pads and nails.

Hindquarters: The hind legs are well boned and muscular through the thigh, with moderate angulation. The hocks are short and turn neither in nor out. In normal stance, the hind legs are parallel to each other from hock to heel and all the joints are in line when viewed from the rear. The rear assembly, in which the rump is slightly higher than the withers, contributes to the breed's unique, springy gait. Dewclaws should be removed. The hind feet fall slightly behind a perpendicular line from the point of buttock when viewed from the side. Hind feet have well arched toes and turn neither in nor out. Pads and nails may be black, white, pink or a combination of these colors. Chocolate dogs may also have brown pads and nails.

Coat: The coat is double, but without the harsh standoff guard hair and woolly undercoat usually associated with double coats. Rather, it is soft and light in texture throughout, though the outer coat carries slightly more weight. The long hair is abundant and, ideally, wavy. An ideal coat will not be so profuse nor overly long as to obscure the natural lines of the dog. Puppies may have a shorter coat. A single, flat coat or an excessively curly coat are equally contrary to type and should be faulted.

Disqualifications:

- *A coarse, wiry coat.*
- *An atypical short coat on an adult dog (atypical would be a smooth, flat coat with, or without furnishings.)*

Color: All colors are acceptable, singly or in any combination. No preference is given to one color over another. The skin may be freckled or parti-colored.

Gait: The Havanese gait is lively, elegant, resilient, and unique, contributing greatly to the breed's overall essential typiness. The characteristic "spring" is caused by the strong rear drive combined with a "flashy" front action effected by the short upper arm. While a truly typey dog is incapable of exaggerated reach and drive, the action does not appear stilted or hackneyed. The slightly higher rear may cause a correctly built specimen to show a flash of pad coming and going. The front legs reach forward freely. There is good extension in the rear and no tendency toward sickle hocks. The topline holds under movement, neither flattening nor roaching. Head carriage is typically high, even on the move.

Temperament: Playful and alert. The Havanese is both trainable and intelligent with a sweet, non-quarrelsome disposition.

Presentation: The dog should be shown as naturally as is consistent with good grooming. He may be shown either brushed or corded. His coat should be clean and well conditioned. In mature specimens, the length of the coat may cause it to fall to either side down the back but it should not appear to be artificially parted. The long, untrimmed head furnishings may fall forward over the eyes, naturally and gracefully to either side of the skull, or held in two small braids beginning above the outer corner of the eyes, secured with plain elastic bands. (No ribbons or bows are permitted.) Corded coats will naturally separate into wavy sections in young dogs, and will in time develop into cords. Adult corded dogs will be completely covered with a full coat of tassle-like cords. In either coat, minimal trimming of the hair at the inside corner of the eye is allowed for hygienic purposes only, and not in an attempt to resculpt the planes of the head. Minimal trimming around the anal and genital areas, for hygienic purposes only, is permissible but should not be noticeable on presentation. The hair on the feet and between the pads should be neatly trimmed for the express purpose of a tidy presentation. Any other trimming or sculpting of the coat is to be so severely penalized as to preclude placement. Because correct gait is essential to breed type, the Havanese is presented at natural speed on a loose lead.

Faults: The foregoing description is that of the ideal Havanese. Any deviation from the above-described dog must be penalized to the extent of the deviation keeping in mind the importance of the contribution of the various features toward the "original purpose of the breed."

Disqualifications:
- *Height at withers under 8 ½ or over 11 ½ inches except that the minimum height range shall not apply to dogs or bitches under twelve months of age.*
- *Complete absence of black (or chocolate in the chocolate dog) pigmentation on the eyerims, nose or lips*
- *Coarse, wiry coat.*
- *An atypical short coat on an adult. (Atypical refers to a smooth, flat coat with, or without furnishings.)*

Did You Know....

Out of 150 AKC breeds, the Havanese is the *only* breed whose standard calls for a topline that is "straight but not level, rising slightly from withers to rump"?

Did You Know.....

The Havanese is the *only* breed in the AKC that allows for parti-colored corded dogs? All the others which allow cording are solid-colored breeds.

The Havanese topline and gait are both unique.

"topline is straight but not level, rising slightly from withers to rump..."

"...springy gait is flashy rather than far-reaching and unique to the breed. "

Chapter 2

Havanese Ownership....
Is it Right For YOU?

Do Your Homework First!

The Havanese is, without a doubt, a delightful little dog. Those who are lucky enough to share their home with one will attest to the charm, intelligence, and intuitive nature of these little Cuban ragmops. Virtually unknown in the US a decade ago, the Havanese is now one of the fastest-growing breeds in the country (surely a double-edged sword for any breed), largely because their size and temperament makes them adaptable to many types of households.

But adding a dog to your household is a long-term commitment, and before you decide this is the perfect breed for you, it is best to do your homework. Small dogs like Havanese can easily live fifteen years or more, and during that time the dog will be a full-fledged member of the family.

How enjoyable and rewarding those years are largely depends upon three things:

1. selecting the right breed in the first place,

2. selecting the right breeder, and

3. selecting the right puppy from its litter for your family.

Let's look at them one by one:

Selecting the Right Breed

In recent years, the popularity of purebreds has risen dramatically, and with good reason. There are over 150 different breeds now registered with the American Kennel Club. Each was developed over many years for a specific purpose, and each has its own unique set of physical and temperamental characteristics. These unique characteristics, which set one breed apart from another, are collectively referred to as *breed type.* By studying breed type, thoughtful buyers can choose a breed whose looks, size, exercise requirements, temperament, and individual needs best suit their own lifestyle.

What is Havanese breed type? (In other words, what makes a Havanese a Havanese?) The AKC Havanese Standard describes a small sturdy dog of immense charm, slightly longer than tall, covered in a profuse, untrimmed mantle of long, silky, wavy hair, with a topline that rises slightly from withers to rump. His head carriage is high, and his plume of a tail is carried arched over his back. His eyes are almond-shaped; his expression is mischievous; his gait is elegant and springy. His character is described as essentially playful rather than decorative, and the overall impression of the dog is one of agility rather than excessive ability to cover ground.

These few phrases from the Standard describe breed type pretty well and provide many clues about the breed that can help you determine if it is indeed the right breed for you.

The Havanese is small, which makes him easy to travel with and adaptable to apartment living, but this small size also makes him, like all other toy breeds, unsuitable as a pet for very young children. Playful, sturdy and a natural lover of children, if raised with them, the Havanese is better with older children than preschoolers because of his size. (Families with active children under 7 years or so would do better to look at the more placid members of the Sporting and Working groups, who are better-equipped to deal with the occasional roughness of very young children without becoming understandably defensive.)

The Havanese coat needs a fair amount of care to keep it healthy and tangle-free even if kept in a puppy-trim; if one doesn't enjoy brushing, this is definitely *not* the right dog to own. Developed in the tropics, the light, silky coat has little insulation against cold and dampness - this is a full-time housedog, and although he may enjoy an outdoor romp, he *cannot* be kept outdoors.

His playful temperament comes with a downside as well - Havanese *do not* do well when left alone for extended periods. They are extremely social little dogs, not content to sleep on the couch in solitude day after day while the owners are gone, and they will become bored and often develop separa-

The Havanese is an agile and athletic dog.

tion anxiety, both of which lead to behavioral problems. **Households in which no one is home for the better part of each day are not really suited to the Havanese.**

This playful nature (remember the mischievous expression!) also precludes the possibility of a dog who will sit endlessly on the lap of a sedentary owner - Havanese, especially young ones, will invent their own games out of boredom and they may not be to the owner's liking!

The words "agility rather than excessive ability to cover ground " are another clue to the Havanese character. Although they can get adequate exercise without the benefit of acres of lawn, those who feel a dog's place indoors is on the floor will not fare well with this breed. These agile little dogs think furniture was designed for their personal comfort, and there is no use trying to change their minds about it.

Dispelling a Few Myths

One often reads that the Havanese is a non-shedding, odorless, hypoallergenic breed, and some buyers are attracted to them primarily for those reasons. It is important to know, before purchasing an expensive Havanese puppy, that none of these statements are entirely true.

All dogs shed. The hair of all mammals, including man, goes through three cycles - anagen (growth), telagen (resting), and catogen (shedding). The length of each cycle (which ultimately determines the length of the hair) is genetically determined, and also influenced by daylight and temperature. Long-haired breeds like the Havanese simply shed each hair *less often* than short-haired breeds. Potential buyers need to be aware that *all* normal dogs will shed hair to some degree and, if this is unacceptable, they need to reconsider adding a dog of any breed other than the Xoloitzcuintli to their household.

No dog is entirely odorless. The familiar "doggy" odor that many find objectionable is caused by an oily substance called *sebum,* produced by the sebaceous glands just beneath the skin. All dogs produce sebum, some more than others. Breeds like retrievers, developed for water work, have notably oily coats, and a stronger doggy odor. Havanese are a relatively "dry" breed - they are not particularly waterproof, and have less odor than many other breeds, but all dogs produce sebum. Regular bathing and grooming will keep the Havanese relatively odor-free, but that is largely the responsibility of the owner.

The Havanese cannot be tolerated by everyone with dog allergies. Most people who are allergic to dogs react to dander, which is the normal sloughing of the outer layer of the skin. Havanese, as do all dogs, produce dander, although not in great amounts.

Those who are allergic to dog saliva will do no better with the Havanese than with any other breed- in some cases they will do worse, because Havanese like to give kisses!

It is true that because they shed less, and produce less dander than many breeds, people who are mildly allergic to dog hair and dander can often tolerate Havanese better than many other breeds, but *hypoallergenic does not mean non-allergenic.* If one has allergies, it would be wise to spend a few hours with a Havanese *several times* before bringing one Into the household, as an allergic reaction may not be produced after a single encounter. It is heartbreaking, and unfair to the puppy, to find out after he has become part of the family that he triggers allergies. Remember, Havanese must be full-time housedogs, and are happy only when in close proximity to the rest of the family. To relegate him to another part of the house, or the outdoors, because a family member has dog allergies amounts to cruelty, and should not even be considered.

Shorthaired Havanese

Occasionally, a Havanese puppy will show up in a litter with an atypical coat. An experienced breeder will recognize them before they are old enough to be placed in their new homes, but a novice breeder may not which inevitably results in consternation on the part of the owner as the dog matures. This is not a result of cross-breeding, or genetic "impurity", but rather an accident of nature. These pups, referred to by breeders as Short-hairs, actually develop adult coats like that of a spaniel, with a smooth muzzle and paws, slightly longer body coat and moderate silky furnishings on the ears, tail and legs. Although disqualified from AKC conformation shows, they may compete in Obedience and Agility events. Perfectly normal in every other way, they make fine pets and are quite cute, although they have a decidedly different "look".

Shorthaired pups are usually sold by responsible breeders for pet price on spay/neuter contracts, and they may appeal to the pet owner who doesn't want to deal with grooming the typical abundant Havanese coat. They are not particularly rare, and under *no circumstances* should they be advertised at inflated prices as "Rare Shorthaired Havanese".

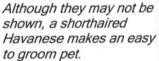

Although they may not be shown, a shorthaired Havanese makes an easy to groom pet.

Miniature or "Teacup" Havanese

Recently, ads have started popping up on the internet for "Miniature" and "Teacup" Havanese, at fairly exorbitant prices. *There is NO SUCH THING as a Miniature Havanese!!!*

The Havanese Standard allows for a height range of 8 ½ to 11 ½ inches at the shoulder, which encompasses a fair amount of variance. (For many years the Standard also included a weight range of 7-13 lbs, although a male of sturdy bone and correct proportion at the high end of the Standard may easily weigh 15 lbs. Unless he is very tall, a Havanese weighing 20-25 lbs or more is usually an achondroplastic dwarf.) Occasionally, a breeding between two dogs of average size may produce a tiny yet healthy Havanese of 7-8 inches and 6-7 lbs, but ethical breeders generally do not breed these dogs, as they fall below the Standard.

Often, however, extremely small size in a Havanese can be indicative of liver or kidney dysfunction, and a puppy that is less than 2 lbs at 9-10 weeks should have a complete blood panel performed by the breeder (including pre- and post-prandial bile acid assays) to exclude the possibility of any congenital defects before sale. An unusually tiny Havanese may very well be healthy, but if it is not, there is heartbreak down the road for the new owner.

Ethical breeders may well produce an occasional tiny puppy, just as they occasionally produce an oversized one, out of parents of correct size, and if one or the other is your preference, you would do well to explain that to breeders out the gate, and they will generally be pleased to sell you one as a pet, to be spayed or neutered (and at pet price!), should they happen to have one pop up in a litter. But ethical breeders *do not* intentionally produce dogs of a size unacceptable in the Havanese Standard by breeding two of them together! Breeders enamored of dogs significantly larger or smaller than the Havanese Standard dictates should seriously consider a different breed altogether, as breeding what one "likes" with no regard for a Standard is a form of arrogance that undermines the integrity of the entire sport of purebred dogs.

Adult or Puppy?

There is no doubt that every Havanese puppy is adorable, and most people think automatically of a puppy when they are considering the addition of a dog to the household.

Those little bundles of fluff, however, require a lot more work than an adult dog. Housebreaking in the small breeds is rarely accomplished in a week or two - it may be several months before a puppy is reliable. They are less flexible in their schedules than adult dogs and they will need early socialization and training. Puppies have a lot of energy and simply require more time than adult dogs for the first year or two. It is also impossible to guarantee, with total certainty, what a puppy will develop into, both size and personality-wise. Will he be bigger than you had hoped? More active, or less? A puppy is all promise and potential, but without a crystal ball, even the best breeder cannot predict exactly how a puppy will turn out. For these reasons, many households would do better with an adult dog, especially the more mature owner, who may find raising a puppy daunting.

Both puppies and adult Havanese adapt easily to new homes.

One of the main concerns most people have about an adult is whether or not the dog will "bond" with a new owner or family. This is not generally a problem for Havanese. The breed is remarkably adaptable and, although they are very social and very affectionate, they are not, as a group, particularly loyal to a single person. Most well-socialized Havanese have the ability to adapt easily to a new home and environment within a matter of weeks, even at five or more years of age.

In fact, retired dogs from a reputable breeder can make some of the best pets. As the Havanese can easily live 15 years or more, these dogs are often the best choice for the person looking for companionship but not quite up to raising a puppy.

If they are from a top-notch breeder, these adult dogs are often champions and have been extensively screened for genetic disorders and other health problems. Because they have been show dogs, they are well-socialized, used to meeting strangers, traveling and being groomed, and are both crate-trained and housebroken. Many breeders will sell these dogs for the same price as a pet-quality puppy because they want them to retire to loving homes, and, unlike a pet-quality puppy, there are no surprises down the road. With an adult, what you see is what you get.

If you think about it, these adult dogs were the pick of their litters, because that is what good breeders keep for themselves. Neutering them and placing them in good homes after they have had a litter or two allows breeders to make room for the next generation of young hopefuls, while giving the dogs a well-deserved retirement in the lap of luxury after having made their contribution to the breed in the show-ring or whelping box.

In the Havanese breed, adult dogs are rarely advertised, however, so if you decide that an adult might best fit your lifestyle, it is a good idea to mention it to breeders you contact right at the outset. One can also contact the Havanese Club of America, which may be able to refer the buyer to available adult dogs from reputable breeders.

Male or Female?

Many people automatically assume that a female dog is more affectionate and less territorial than a male, but in the Havanese breed, quite the opposite is often true.

If you come out and ask, nearly every breeder will tell you it is the male Havanese who is more likely to sit on your lap, and to follow you around the house while you are going about your daily routine. The females are often more independent. No one knows why this is, but as a general rule, the male Havanese is simply more affectionate.

The Havanese breed as a whole is not particularly territorial and, again, the males tend to be *less* so than the females. Havanese males are not quarrelsome as a general rule and, in many households, two males can live together in absolute harmony. In fact, it is the females who will be more likely to jockey for position in the family "pack".

If one is looking for a companion, and planning to spay or neuter (spayed and neutered pets live longer, healthier lives and are at less risk for several forms of cancer) the decision on whether to get a male or a female should be based on the personality of the individual puppy itself rather than the gender. An experienced breeder will try to find the puppy in the litter that best fits your family's needs and lifestyle, and being open-minded about its gender will actually make that job easier.

Selecting the Right Breeder

Many people spend a lot of time researching the right breed for their family and then, assuming all breeders are equal, purchase a puppy based primarily upon price and availability. This is all too often an unfortunate mistake and can have disastrous consequences.

All breeders are *not* the same, and all puppies are not of equal quality just because they are purebred. In the Havanese breed, the unwary buyer will often pay as much or more for a poor-quality pup than for a well-bred one.

In the last few years, the internet has radically changed the way we buy and sell dogs. Buyers are no longer limited to those dogs available at their local pet shops or advertised in their local paper. A click of the mouse will produce literally *hundreds* of breeders worldwide in any breed, and that in itself can be daunting. As breeders go, the Good, the Bad, and the Ugly are all out there in cyberspace together.

In today's internet world, serious hobby show-breeders, well-meaning, but uneducated, backyard breeders, and outright puppy mills all have websites, and it is often hard to know the difference until it is too late. What's a puppy-buyer to do?

The American Kennel Club's website at www.akc.org is a great starting point for anyone researching purebred dogs. In addition, each breed's AKC Parent Club has a website full of information about their breed, easily accessible through AKC. **The Parent Club's website should be *the first stop* for anyone researching any breed.**

Why visit the Parent Club website first? Each AKC breed has a Parent Club - like the AKC, each organization is *a not-for-profit corporation* comprised of members who have a mandate, defined in their Club's Constitution, to both further and protect the interests of their breed at the national level. All breeders' personal websites, no matter how informative, are in reality "infomercials" - that is why they end in *.com* (as in *commercial*) rather than *.org* (as in *organization.*)

The Havanese Club of America, the AKC Parent Club for the Havanese, has an excellent website at www.havanese.org. It contains a wealth of information for the potential and new owner, including current health information about the breed. It lists local Havanese clubs, and upcoming events that may be scheduled in your area where you can meet lots of Havanese and their owners. The HCA also maintains a breeder referral list. These breeders are HCA members who have met the standards set forth by the HCA Buyer's Education Committee, and breeders who cannot provide documentation of health-screening on the parents of an upcoming litter are ineligible to be listed. Studying the information on the HCA's website will quickly turn you into an educated buyer and can save you a lot of heartbreak down the road.

The educated buyer knows beforehand what to look for on a breeder's website, and knows what questions to ask the breeder. He listens carefully to the answers, and accepts no excuses. Serious hobby breeders are aware of the health problems in the breed and can provide certification that their breeding stock has been screened for nearly all hereditary problems. Many list this information on their personal websites.

Virtually all health-screening can now be verified at www.offa.org, where the Orthopedic Foundation for Animals, in cooperation with the AKC Canine Health Foundation, maintains an extensive cross-listed database referred to as CHIC (Canine Health Information Center), and it is a good idea to do so before purchase. If a dog is not listed, *it has not been certified,* no matter *what* the breeder says.

Good breeders are familiar with the Havanese Standard and breed to produce pups displaying proper breed type. Many compete with their dogs in AKC conformation events, where breeding dogs are evaluated against the Standard by licensed judges. They will provide "soaped" photographs of the parents upon request (these photographs, taken when the dog is slathered in shampoo, reveal skeletal structure hidden by the coat.)

They evaluate each puppy's structure at eight weeks or so.

They understand the need for health testing and early socialization, and evaluate their puppies' temperaments before making final placement decisions.

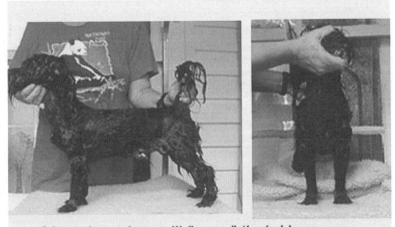

Many breeders will "soap" their Havanese to evaluate structure beneath the coat.

This pup has been soaped up at 8 weeks to evaluate structure

They will gladly provide references. And they will *not* sell you a pup they do not think will be right for your family.

Puppy Aptitude Test

Restraint:
The tester gently rolls the pup on its back and holds it down with light pressure for 30 seconds. This pup is being evaluated for dominance level.

That said, there are "show breeders" and there are "show breeders." An AKC championship alone does not guarantee anything other than that on at least three separate occasions, the dog was considered to conform to the Standard better than any other Havanese shown in the ring with him *on that day*. It does *not* guarantee good health, or even soundness.

Many potential pet owners feel that buying from a serious hobby show-breeder is not important if they are "just looking for a pet". *Nothing could be further from the truth!* A good pet is also a sound and *healthy* pet. Health problems can be expensive, heartbreaking for the pet owner, and painful or even life-threatening for the poor dog. (Ironically, backyard breeders who do not bother to spend the money to health-screen the parents "because they have no problems in their line" are invariably less inclined to stand behind the dog should health problems develop later.) Very few pups produced by experienced breeders "make the grade" as show prospects, as most wish to send only their very best efforts into the ring to represent their line, so the pet puppies produced by serious hobby show-breeders are likely to be of far higher quality than the best puppies produced by well-meaning backyard breeders, who may be caring and kind, but are less knowledgeable about the breed in general.

Buyers should be aware that good breeders often have a waiting list, and that the first puppy available may not always be the best choice in the long run. No matter how anxious you are to add a Havanese to your household, the extra few months it may take to get a dog from a knowledgeable and ethical breeder is very little time when pro-rated over the fifteen or so years you will have the dog. When it comes to buying a Havanese puppy, "instant gratification" most often leads to regret.

What about distance? With the advent of the internet, the buyer can now find a Havanese puppy almost anywhere and, indeed, many internet sites proudly proclaim that they "will ship anywhere". Be advised that most good breeders are unwilling to entrust tiny and vulnerable puppies, into whom they

Young puppies travel well in under-seat carriers

have poured much time and effort, to the vagaries of the airlines as though they were a crate of oranges, and will require the prospective owner to come pick them up. This may seem inconvenient but it is, for many wise breeders, a measure of the buyer's willingness to make a long-term and serious commitment to dog ownership and a willingness to inconvenience oneself, if need be, for the safety and well-being of the puppy. If the potential buyer finds it too expensive or inconvenient to come get his puppy, what other future facets of ownership that affect the dog's safety and well-being will he find too expensive or inconvenient ?

Physically picking up one's own puppy is actually a safeguard for the buyer as well, especially if one is buying via the internet where, frankly, anyone can look good. **Beware the breeder who will not allow you to pick up the puppy, or who offers to meet you at a more "convenient location" - there may well be a good reason he or she does not want you to visit the premises!** A Havanese of any age may be carried home in the passenger compartment of the plane in a pet-carrier right under the seat, so distance is not an issue when looking for the right pup. Discount flights often make this option cheaper than shipping air freight, as well as infinitely safer and less traumatic for the pup.

The best advice when choosing a breeder is to try not to succumb to Puppy Fever. This malady, which affects not dogs but rather buyers, especially when faced with an adorable fluffy puppy available *right now*, causes all common sense to fly out the window and red flags to become virtually invisible. ALL Havanese puppies are adorable. Some of them, through no fault of their own, will *not* grow up to be healthy, happy, and handsome dogs, because they are being produced by people whose sole motive is profit. These people count on Puppy Fever to keep them in business. Please don't help to ensure their future success - if buyers are educated and there is no profitable market for their puppies in pet shops or on the internet, they will have to find another way to make a living, and the world of dogs will be better off.

Selecting the Right Puppy

Selecting the puppy becomes a lot easier when one is dealing with an experienced breeder. These breeders will ask you a lot of questions about your family, your lifestyle, and what you are looking for in a puppy in terms of temperament and color preferences, and then will generally sort out the puppies themselves. When the puppies' future owners all live some distance from the litter, this makes practical sense. The breeder, who has spent innumerable hours with the puppies as they develop, is usually in a better position to evaluate them than a buyer who spends an hour or two with the litter at best, when the most energetic puppy may just be sleepy. Many breeders utilize the Puppy Aptitude Test, (a series of simple exercises performed on each puppy that reveal his degree of dominance/submissiveness, dependence/independence and so forth) as a tool to help match each puppy with the right home.

Many older dog books will tell you to examine the litter, and look for the liveliest puppy, discarding the less-lively immediately. They suggest you perform an amateur veterinary examination of the puppy, checking for discharge from the eyes or nose, etc. These instructions, in truth, are leftover from earlier days when vaccination for diseases like distemper and parvovirus were unavailable, and parasites were everywhere. The liveliest puppies were least likely to have distemper, or a heavy parasite infestation. Good breeders today vaccinate and worm puppies on a predetermined schedule,

Colored collars help the breeder to identify the littermates.

and puppies are given a "well-puppy exam" by the breeder's vet *before* going to their new homes. (Along with the AKC registration application, pedigree, and a sales contract, reputable Havanese breeders will provide you with copies of the puppy's exam, copies of any health-screening such as BAER-testing performed, and a record of worming and vaccination, along with detailed instructions for feeding, future vaccinations, and parasite control.)

However, if you are in a position to visit a litter before purchase, there are things you should be looking for. The puppies should be clean, sweet-smelling, fluffy and socialized, and they should be in a roomy confined area of the house (never a garage or shed!) that is clean and warm, with piddle-pads or a litter box available for their use, soft toys and fresh water available, and soft squishy beds for napping. Some breeders raise puppies in elevated wire pens, which keeps them clean with little work on the breeder's part, but these puppies are often very difficult to housebreak as the early natural instinct to keep their sleeping area dry is never developed. There is *no excuse whatsoever* for dirty, sticky puppies living on newspaper! Breeders who are careless about puppy management are unlikely to be diligent about things like health-testing, parasite control, and general good breeding practices. Unless the puppies are easily identifiable by color, they should have different colored collars so that one may be easily distinguished from another for purposes of weighing, worming, vaccination, and individual socialization.

The adult dogs in the household should be clean, sociable, and well-cared for as well. Ideally, multiple dog households, especially those with intact animals of both genders, will have facilities for those dogs other than a bank of crates stacked floor-to-ceiling along with a few ex-pens providing the only fenced exercise areas, which is generally an indication of poor management and limited resources if nothing else.

Havanese are not lab rats and should not be kept as such merely for purposes of reproduction - each breeding animal needs adequate personal space to sleep and play, toys, intellectual stimulation, and access to spacious safely fenced exercise areas. Refusal to allow you to see the dam of the litter and/or any other dogs in the household, or where those dogs are housed (other than those bitches who may have new litters) should be considered a major red flag, no matter what excuse is given. *Ethical breeders do not hide their breeding stock, nor the area in which they are kept.* A pervasive smell of urine is a red flag as well, as it indicates poor management.

Sometimes show breeders will have a pup or two (3-6 months) that they are "running on". These are promising puppies being evaluated for show potential. If they do not measure up, they are placed as pets, and the lucky pet owner gets a better-than-average pup that may have a minor cosmetic flaw such as an uneven bite or an undescended testicle. Potential show puppies often receive a lot of early attention from the breeder, and are usually well-socialized.

Just Slip Out the Back, Jack...

The most important thing to remember when visiting a breeder and looking at puppies is to trust your instincts. If you are *not comfortable* with the conditions you encounter, it is far better to look elsewhere, even if it means you will lose a deposit. (That deposit might well be a drop in the bucket compared to what you could be spending in vet bills over the next ten years if the pup is unhealthy.)

Many buyers feel "trapped" once they have arrived at the breeder's, and feel obligated to write the check and take the puppy in spite of their misgivings. DON'T DO IT- *that's exactly what these breeders are counting on!* Better to come up with an excuse and just slide on out of there....and any old excuse you can come up with will do. (If you can't come up with a good one, you can always tell them the truth, if you don't mind a confrontation.)

Buying an expensive puppy to "rescue it" from deplorable conditions is *not* a good idea. It will simply help to keep an unethical breeder in business and bring many more owners heartbreak down the road, as well as dooming future puppies into existence.

Bringing Home the Puppy...What is the Best Age?

About thirty years ago, it was discovered that puppies' neurological development was complete at 49 days and, because of this, it was assumed that 7 weeks was the ideal time for puppies to go to their new homes for purposes of early socialization. For puppies the size of Havanese, however, 7 weeks is simply too early. Most experienced breeders like to keep their Havanese puppies until they are at least 9-10 weeks old, when they have had their second set of vaccinations, and been wormed more than once. Show breeders may wish to keep them longer for evaluation purposes. If the breeder is providing adequate socialization at this critical period, nothing is lost there. Beware the breeder who is willing to let you have a puppy who is barely weaned- no matter how anxious you are to bring a puppy home, tiny puppies are high-risk puppies.

A healthy Havanese puppy should ideally weigh at least two pounds before it is sent to its new home, and will more likely be in the 3-4 pound range. Pups significantly smaller than that at 9-10 weeks should be certified clear by the breeder's vet of congenital liver or kidney dysfunction before purchase.

What's This Puppy Going to Cost Me?

Because the demand for Havanese is skyrocketing, the cost of puppies is skyrocketing as well. A well-bred, AKC-registered Havanese pet puppy from a reputable breeder out of completely health-tested parents currently costs between $1,800 and $2,500, and maybe more by the time you read this. Believe it or not, they are losing money on the deal.

Pet-shop puppies are often much *more* expensive than those from reputable show breeders who do all the necessary health-testing, not because they are higher-quality, but simply because pet shops have overhead they need to cover, and they buy their puppies wholesale (from brokers) and sell retail.

The reason ethical breeders do not make money is actually because, unlike pet shops, they haven't figured this wholesale/retail thing out yet... most sell their puppies for below *production cost*, much less wholesale, which is why they need a real job to support their dog-breeding habit. In other words, they do it because they love it. And they *never* figure their time into the equation, because it's too depressing.

No matter *what* the pet shop personnel tells you, "reputable breeders" do NOT supply pet shops!!! Only the absolute bottom-feeders of the dog-breeding world do, and selling pups to a pet shop will get you thrown out of virtually *every* AKC Parent Club, including the HCA. So do not buy into that line....it's a sales tactic, and it's just not true. Ever.

Sometimes one may see "lovingly home-raised" Havanese puppies advertised in the newspaper or the pet magazines for far less, but saving a few hundred dollars to buy a puppy from mediocre "backyard" bloodlines, no matter how "lovingly" they were raised, is rarely a savings in the long run, as these puppies rarely come from health-screened parents, and can end up costing the owner thousands of dollars in orthopedic, eye, or liver surgery within the first year, and too often are poor representatives of their breed.

In short, the actual *cost* of the puppy is less important than whether or not the puppy comes from health-certified parents and a knowledgeable, ethical breeder who is willing to stand behind the puppies they produce with a written contract. The initial purchase price is a very small part of the cost of dog ownership over a 15-year period, and should *never* be the deciding factor.

This 6 week old Havanese weighs 2.5lbs and should be between 3-4 lbs by 9 weeks of age.

Chapter 3

The Right Stuff....or, Buying Out the Store

If the truth be known, successful ownership of a Havanese puppy requires only slightly more equipment than successful ownership of a professional hockey team. Having the "right stuff" will make every aspect of training easier for both the puppy and the rest of the family.

Getting It All Together

Bringing home a new Havanese puppy is like bringing home a new baby- you've got to buy all the stuff you'll need in advance and have the nursery set up *before* the puppy gets there. Besides giving you more time to spend with him, the transition from his breeder's home to yours will be far smoother if the puppy has a place all his own right from the start, set up and ready to go.

A favorite toy can keep a pup out of mischief.

Setting Up the Nursery

This "place of his own" will be the nursery - young puppies, like babies, need to be kept safely confined unless they are being directly supervised. You would not have given your toddler the run of the house when you were not watching him, nor should you consider it with your puppy.

Some owners will block off an entire room, such as the kitchen, as a nursery but, for a 4 pound puppy, this is really too much space for him to start with when unattended, and housebreaking will be more difficult.

The best way to set up a nursery is with *a portable exercise pen.* These pens come in wire or plastic, fold flat for storage, and generally open up into an area roughly 16 square feet in size, (usually 4 X 4, although you can be creative with the configuration if you need to) which is ample for a Havanese puppy. Primarily used by dog show exhibitors, they make an ideal puppy playpen, and show breeders often raise their litters in them.

Portable "ex pens" can be purchased at the pet superstore retailers, or through any of the mail-order dog supply companies. For a Havanese puppy, the ideal puppy playpen is 30 inches high, with a door.

Here two ex-pens have been combined to allow more space for a growing litter. It has room for food/water, sleeping quarters, ample play area and toilet (litter pan).
In the foreground is a "puppy john" which holds piddle pads, another option for indoor potty needs.

The play pen should be set up in an area of the house where the family gathers, like the kitchen or family room, rather than isolated in a laundry room. If the flooring in this area is carpeted or otherwise not accident-proof, a remnant of vinyl flooring, a heavy clear vinyl shower curtain, or a remnant of flannel-backed upholstery vinyl can be purchased inexpensively to go under the play pen. The vinyl sheet flooring can be easily wiped up if an accident happens, and the others can go right into the washer and dryer. (Tossing a white towel and a little bleach into the wash load on warm, and drying both on the delicate cycle, works remarkably well.)

Remember, you do *not* want to isolate your puppy in a low-traffic area of the house - the dog is a pack animal, and for pack animals with strong social needs, isolation is the worst form of torture. This play pen, which will serve as the nursery, should have everything in it that a puppy needs for several unsupervised hours:

- A soft fluffy bed for napping. This can be placed inside a crate with the door securely fastened open, or it can be a donut-style bed with soft cuddly sides.

Puppies love the security of a donut bed.

- A litter box and /or a "puppy piddle pad" and frame so that the puppy can relieve himself in an acceptable place if no one is around to let him out.

- A water-bottle such as those used for rabbits attached to the side of the pen, which will keep fresh water handy with no accidental spillage.

- A spill-proof food dish if you plan to feed him in his nursery, which is a good idea. (Make sure the food dish is as far from the bathroom area as possible.) *Lots* of toys and a couple chewy things for teething. It's a good idea to rotate the toys in the playpen to avoid boredom.

A well equipped ex-pen provides a safe playpen for your puppy.

A painted concrete block with holes in it, or a large drainage tile, will make a good "gymnasium" addition to the playpen, and will keep the puppy occupied, as Havanese puppies love to climb over and through things.

With this setup, a puppy can be safely left unsupervised for several hours each day, if need be when no one is home, and can also be "with the family" when everyone *is* home, without being directly underfoot. There are times when this is a good idea - just as too little stimulation is detrimental to a young puppy, too much can be exhausting for him, especially in an active home with children. Puppies, like everyone else, need a little space sometimes. When your puppy is loose, it is very important to leave the door of his playpen open so he has access to his "bathroom facilities", in [ ] should he need to use them.

The puppy nursery can be used as long as needed. Some owners continue to use it when the dog is an adult, seeing it as a roomier alternative to crating when no one is home for extended periods during the day, rather like having his own "condo". If your Havanese is a climber, a specially-fitted top can be purchased to keep him in.

"Puppy Stuff" Checklist

Portable exercise pen

Soft dog bed

Litter pan and litter

Puppy pads and frame

Two spillproof dishes

Water bottle

Soft collar and lead

Stuffed toys

Chew toys

Small biscuits or dog treats

Travel bag

Grooming supplies

To Crate or Not to Crate?

A crate is *not* a cage, and should not be viewed as one. The domestic dog inherited from his wolf ancestors strong den-dwelling instincts and, if properly introduced and not abused, your Havanese will view his crate as his den throughout his life.

This litter is being raised with a crate, minus its door, as sleeping quarters so they will be well used to being in a crate when they leave for their new homes.

A crate should never, *ever*, be used as punishment and a puppy should never be locked in a crate when no one is around to let him out if he needs to relieve himself. Dogs have a strong instinct to prevent soiling their dens and, once that instinct is overridden by necessity, housebreaking becomes a much greater challenge. Young Havanese puppies have a maximum bladder capacity of about a *teaspoonful* on a good day and, while a crate is a great housebreaking tool for a large sporting breed, it's not ideal for Toy breed puppies. The playpen, with its "indoor bathroom" facilities is, by far, the better option and will result in more successful housebreaking.

So why bother with a crate at all? A dog who is conditioned positively to a crate early on will accept riding or sleeping in one with much less fuss than a dog who has not been conditioned early, and there are many times throughout a dog's life when a crate is essential. A dog the size of an adult

Havanese should *never* ride loose in a car any more than one would allow a ten-pound infant to ride unprotected, and for the same reasons - even a minor impact can turn the dog into a projectile missile, and the landing can be fatal. A well-made crate is the *only* safe "car seat" for a Havanese.

In addition to riding in cars, a small crated dog is accepted in many of the better hotel chains and is a more welcome guest in a private home. All dogs should be crated in vet's offices, *especially* puppies - face it, a lot of sick dogs pass through there and a pup is less exposed to viruses and bacteria that may be floating around if he's snug in his own crate than he would be snuffling around on the waiting room floor on the end of a leash.

As an adult, a Havanese who has been properly conditioned to a crate will often seek out his "den" when he feels like a nap, or just wants some time on his own. (The crate door should always be open for this reason, and the crate should be in an accessible location.) Children should be taught to respect this and never bother the dog when he's napping in his crate. Some Havanese sleep in their crates at night all their lives, especially those in multiple-dog households and some eat in their crates, which is a good idea.

Some Havanese puppies will sleep happily in their playpen in the family room at night, while others will howl pitifully out of loneliness, depending upon their individual level of independence. (This dependence/independence thing is pre-installed hardware, by the way, and there's not much you can do about it.) Mr. Lonely will be much happier sleeping in the bedroom, closer to his new human pack members. The neediest puppies will want their crate on a chair right next to the bed. After making sure his miniscule bladder is empty, he can be popped cheerfully into the crate with a little biscuit and a pat on the head (a puppy should always receive a food reward when he goes into his crate for successful conditioning) and he should be settled in just fine until he feels the need to go potty, which will probably be sometime around 2 AM, in which case you need to get up and take him either outside or to his litterbox, depending on the weather and your own personal preference. By twelve or fourteen weeks, or so, a Havanese puppy should be able to make it through the night.

Whether the puppy initially spends the night in his crate or in his play-pen, crate-training should be started early. The puppy should be allowed to take naps in his crate (when someone is home) and should be taken either outside or to his litter box immediately upon waking up, so that he learns where the accepted places are to eliminate.

There are essentially two kinds of crates to consider - wire fold-downs and the plastic kind, with a wire-mesh door, which now come in a variety of colors. (The most popular solid crate is probably the VariKennel 100, which will fit most Havanese.) Some dogs, again depending on their tempera-ment, prefer the better views afforded by a wire crate, and some prefer the snugness of the solid ones. You might as well get one of each- all real "dog people" have a couple extra crates around at all times, as one never knows when they'll be needed. Both need crate pads, and the options here are endless- just make sure they are soft, machine washable and can go in the dryer.

The other main option in crates is the soft-sided airline crate. These are wonderful and will be discussed later. You'll definitely need one, but it can-not be the dog's primary crate, as they won't stand up to daily use.

Litter Boxes, Puppy pads, and Other Toiletries

Surely one of the best inventions of the last few years, especially for

small breeds like the Havanese, is dog litter. These pellets, made from recycled paper and used in a litter pan designed especially for dogs, have simply revolution-ized housebreaking. Both the litter and the pans are available at most major pet superstores, and a few of the dog supply cata-logues are now carrying them.

Successful housebreaking depends entirely upon the ability to praise the puppy when he eliminates in the "right" area, and to quickly correct him *each and every time* he begins to eliminate in the "wrong" area, with a quick "ACK!" to catch his attention and stop the process while getting him to the "right" one in a hurry in order to finish the job. With a puppy the size of the Havanese, the sheer frequency of elimination makes this a nearly insurmountable challenge for the owner. Dog litter changes all that.

Litter training is a boon to apartment dwellers and a Havanese can easily adapt back and forth, using both the outdoors and the litter box. This is a great help in inclement weather when many adult Havanese would prefer not to brave the elements and appreciate "indoor facilities" as much as anyone else. Many Havanese breeders have begun using dog litter for their puppies, over the last few years, and recommend that the owners continue with it. Puppies trained to pads or paper by the breeder can easily be taught to use litter by initially lining the box with the surface he is used to, and adding litter gradually until the transition is complete.

An alternative to litter are puppy "piddle pads", absorbent pads made of the same stuff as disposable diapers. Their disadvantage is that puppies are inclined to shred them as a form of entertainment and they are best used with the little plastic frames that hold them in place. Their main advantage is that they are easily folded into the pocket of a soft-sided carrying bag, and are indispensable in emergencies. (On a long airline flight, for example, a puppy pad can be spread out on the floor of the loo, saving a puppy from soiling his carrier.)

Whether you use a litter box or a piddle pad, the technique for housebreaking is the same - take the puppy to the desired area to eliminate immediately upon his waking up and after eating, and praise him lavishly when he uses it. Consistency is the key to success. Bear in mind, though, that a Havanese is rarely reliably housebroken before six months of age, and some are closer to a year. Knowing this in advance will keep you from getting discouraged or thinking you are doing something wrong. Odds are you're not.

Intact males will sometimes lift their legs indoors, usually on corners or furniture - this is *not* a housebreaking issue!! What they are doing is marking their territory by leaving their scent and will most often do it when there are bitches around. It's a very basic canine behavior, and has more to do with establishing dominance than with testosterone, as dominant Havanese bitches will also mark territory - some will actually lift their leg! Neutered males will also sometimes mark if they are especially dominant and/or live in a multiple-dog household. (Single dogs are much less likely to mark, even intact males, than dogs who have other dogs around.) Dogs who will not mark in their own house because they have been corrected for it will often embarrass their owners by trying it in other people's homes, or in hotel rooms - if the home belongs to an experienced "dog person", they will probably be understanding; on the other hand, your mother-in-law may not be quite so amused!

One sure-fire way of preventing this is by purchasing "bad-boy pants", which are essentially a cloth band with a Velcro closure that wraps around the male dog's groin area. A feminine hygiene pad fits on the underside to catch any social errors on the dog's part, so he can lift his leg with cheery abandon without doing any damage. Bitches who mark, or those in heat, can be fitted with specially-made panties as well. Both are pretty easy to put on and take off (make sure you remove them before the dog goes outside!) and there are times when they will simply save you aggravation.

One more caveat in the housebreaking department - Havanese puppies need to have the hair under the tail and around the anus trimmed regularly, or the feces will get stuck in the hair, and the puppy will not be able to eliminate. If the breeder has not already done so, make sure you do it when the puppy arrives. Often when a puppy is straining, with no result, that is the reason why.

The Great Outdoors

The Havanese is first and foremost a house dog, but they do enjoy the outdoors provided the weather is fine. Ideally, if one has a yard, it should be securely fenced, either partially or completely, and absolutely escape-proof.

Swimming pools must be off-limits - if the pool itself is not fenced, a Havanese *cannot* be left unsupervised in the yard, as they will surely jump in and be unable to get out unassisted. An otherwise intelligent breed, Havanese are not bright in this regard. Even ornamental garden ponds can be a major hazard to Havanese puppies.

Outdoor fencing should be sturdy, escape-proof, and at least 3-4 feet high. Privacy fencing (which limits barking at the dog next door) and picket both work well; chain-link, which now comes in green and black as well as the classically unattractive galvanized gray, is the time-honored choice for all dogs.

If one's lawn is unfenced, the dog *must* be walked on a leash, even in the dark and when it's raining. Consider it good exercise for both of you. If your backyard is fenced, but the front is not, you need to train your Havanese never to go out the front door. (The safest course of action is to either fence the front yard as well and add a gate, or limit his access to the front door entirely.) Many a dog has been lost or killed outright by scooting out the front door while the owner is trying to get rid of a door-to-door salesman.

A note on invisible fencing: Although Havanese are easily capable of learning to stay within the confines of an invisible fence, it is not a good idea for *any* small breed, as they are completely vulnerable to large dogs who may wander in, attack, and even kill them. An invisible fence will keep your dog *in*, but it won't keep strange dogs *out*, and if the electronics malfunction, you have no fence. A false sense of security is worse than no security at all. *Don't even consider it.* Many Havanese breeders will not sell a pup to a home with an invisible fence.

Dog Beds, Dog Beds, Dog Beds...

A Havanese cannot have too many dog beds. Donut beds, igloo beds, beanbag-style beds, beds that look like miniature pieces of furniture - they love them all, and will claim them all as their own property. Once your Havanese is old enough to have the run of the house, he will appreciate a dog bed of his own in every room, including the bathroom. All colors, styles, and

fabrics are acceptable, as long as they can be thrown into the wash and machine-dried. Puppies especially prefer donut-style beds, as the soft round sides allow for a feeling of security. Do not think for a minute that an extensive collection of the finest dog beds will keep your Havanese off the furniture, though. It won't.

Food Dishes and Water Bottles

The array of dining accoutrements for dogs available in catalogues and stores is somewhat daunting. There are more possibilities than imaginable, and all have their place somewhere in the world of dogs. Crockery, stainless steel, plastic, even little raised "double-doggy diners" are all available - the question is, which is right for the Havanese?

As Havanese are inclined to be picky eaters and play with both their food and their dishes, a heavy ceramic or stainless "spill-proof" dish is the probably the best idea for both food and water, as it discourages carrying them around if nothing else. The ones that are labeled as dishwasher-safe are best, and should be washed frequently.

One of the best ideas to come along for small dogs is the hanging water-bottle designed for rabbits and hamsters. Both puppies and adults quickly learn to use them, and they provide clean fresh water at all times. They prevent both spills and wet drippy faces resulting from dunking their facial furnishings in the water bowl. On lighter-colored dogs this will help prevent the unattractive staining around the muzzle caused by a constantly wet face. In addition, they tend to prevent a puppy-problem known as 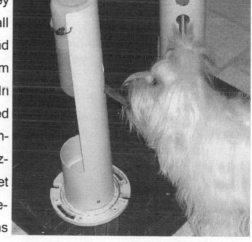 "tanking up." (Puppies, like babies, will drink until they are *tired* rather than until their thirst is satiated. A puppy can drink quite a bit of water before he actually gets tired, and excessive consumption when faced with a full water-bowl will slow down the housebreaking process. Frequent, smaller drinks from a water bottle will prevent this.) When traveling, a hamster-sized water bottle attached to the crate door will allow the dog access to water without a mess. A plastic crate cup beneath the bottle will catch any drips. For adult dogs who don't need a play pen, a water bottle on a free-standing unit can be purchased and placed in a corner of the kitchen.

Dog Toys and Chewy Things

Like beds, a Havanese cannot own too many toys. To a dog, their preference is for soft stuffed toys over latex, although no one knows why. Small puppies appreciate very little stuffed toys, which are easily carried, and these often remain favorites even when they are grown. Interactive toys, into which treats are inserted, are often not favorites for the simple reason that Havanese, as a breed, are praise-motivated rather than food-motivated. The ubiquitous Kong, 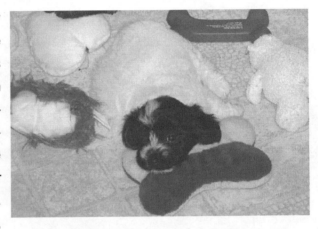 for which many breeds of dogs will perform feats of amazing heroism such as detecting bombs on airplanes, elicits little or no interest from the average Havanese. The same is true of nylon bones. On the other hand, stuffed toys that squeak, bark, burp, or otherwise make stupid noises absolutely knock them out- Havanese for some reason simply *adore* them.

Teething Havanese puppies need to satisfy their need to chew; in fact, chew toys are essential to healthy teeth and gums throughout a dog's life. In the wild, gnawing on bones usually with the raw hide still attached kept the dog's teeth clean, and this is still true today, but care must be taken to choose the *right* bones and rawhide. Commercially available large natural bones and medium-sized tied rawhide bones are by far the safest and, even then, common sense must be used. Choking is a hazard with *any* bone or chewy thing where small pieces can be chewed off, or when the object itself gets small enough to fit in the dog's mouth. Large, thick rawhide chips work well for a dog the size of Havanese, and as they are inexpensive, they may be replaced as soon as they get sufficiently chewed around the edges to present a choking hazard or they become unattractively grubby. Small or thin chips of any kind are decidedly unsafe. Pig's ears are generally safe, and popular with Havanese but they are, not surprisingly, greasy, can stain carpeting and furniture, and may upset dogs' stomachs. (Lamb's ears, which are harder to find, are a better choice.) *Any* chew toys made of compressed flaked material, dyed, and formed into cute shapes can break off in chunks and present a serious choking hazard - they are best avoided. "Natural" chews, like large bones, large rawhide, hooves, cow's tails, "bully" sticks (trust me, you don't want to *know!*) and other assorted "parts" are generally safer, although the owner may find them slightly disgusting.

The Well-Dressed Havanese

Every Havanese needs a soft collar with a tag including his name and phone number, and he should wear it at all times unless he is actually in the bathtub or under general anesthesia. The soft braided nylon works best for small puppies, as they are infinitely adjustable. (Some owners are afraid to put a dog's name on his collar, but this is sheer nonsense. Far more dogs are lost than deliberately stolen, and a lost dog is comforted by a stranger knowing his name. A phone number on a tag will do more to insure his return should he become lost than anything else.)

Many owners of adult Havanese prefer a rolled leather collar, as it is reportedly less likely to tangle the hair, while others prefer soft nylon with a snap release, which is easier to get on and off for bathing and grooming. Harnesses are not recommended, as these little dogs can easily learn to walk on a lead with a collar with a little practice, and a harness will tangle a Havanese coat into mats in a New York minute. (So will a collar, for that matter, but just in *less places*. Remove the collar before his daily brushing, and make sure any tangles forming around the neck area are brushed out thoroughly before putting it back on.)

All Havanese need to learn to walk on a lead, and again, the choices here are soft nylon or leather. A six-foot lead is more than adequate.

The 15 foot retractable lead has become popular in recent years, and it is fine in a few situations - deserted soccer fields and one's own unfenced backyard come to mind, assuming one has no trees or other obstacles. Retractable leads are highly dangerous for both dogs and people in high-traffic or congested areas, however, and they do not teach a dog much about leash-training. If you choose to use one, be considerate of others and be sure the dog is leash-trained *first*.

The other article of "Havanese wear" you might want to consider, especially if you live in a wet climate and need to walk your dog, is a doggy-sized raincoat. As Havanese get soaked in a hurry, this is actually more practical than silly. The yellow slickers are particularly cool- makes 'em look like they belong on a box of frozen fish sticks.

Pet Action Shots

A clean, healthy, well socialized Havanese puppy, pretty as a picture!

Chapter 4

Getting Off to a Good Start or ...

How to Survive the First Few Months

Bringing a new dog into the family is a lot like adding a child - you, the owner, will be responsible for his health, safety, well-being, and education for many years. As with children, early education has many benefits, and that education starts the minute you bring him home. Consider the information in this chapter Havanese Head Start...

Picking Up Your New Puppy

If at all possible, it is best to plan the actual "puppy pick-up" so that the puppy spends his first night away from his littermates in his new home rather than a strange hotel. Doing what one needs to in order to keep a lonely puppy quiet in a motel room (which often comes down to letting the puppy sleep on the bed!) will do nothing to make the *second* night any oas ier, and you will have started off on the wrong foot. You don't want to confuse the puppy, and if he thinks the motel room is the new home for which he left his mom and littermates, you cannot blame him for being unimpressed. If you have a long drive that involves a single overnight stay, plan it so that you stay in a nearby motel the night *before* you pick up the pup.

If you *cannot* manage it without an overnight stay on the way home as well, seriously consider flying - it is far less stressful for the puppy. (The overwhelming majority of pups are quieter, and less likely to suffer motion sickness, under the seat of a plane, even a small one, than they are in a car - I have no idea why. They require no sedation whatsoever, and don't let anyone talk you into it.)

You will need to bring lots of stuff with you for the trip, of course - a crate or carrier, bedding for it, toys, chewies, a water-bottle (fill it at the breeder's or use bottled water) and a small water dish if it's a soft-sided bag.

A roll of paper towels and baby wipes can come in handy, as will a piddle pad or two for stops. It is also a good idea to bring a small towel or toy to rub over his mom and/or littermates - dogs have remarkable olfactory memory, and things that smell like home will be comforting.

Unless the trip is more than 6 hours or so, feeding him enroute is not a great idea. Dogs are naturally disinclined to eat when traveling - unlike humans, who regularly nosh their way cross country - and this is probably a good instinct. (It is a good idea to bring a little food along in a baggie, however, in case you get "stuck." Make sure it is the brand the puppy is currently eating.)

One more caveat for the ride home - if you stop at a wayside, avoid the areas that say "Dog Exercise Area" - that's where all the germs are! It's safer to choose an out-of the way spot, and take your chances with the local Gendarmes.

"Puppy Pick-Up Trip" Checklist

Crate or soft carrier
Towel for bedding
Second towel for bedding
Paper towels
Baby wipes
Air freshener for the car
Small plastic trash bags
Bottled water
Soft toy or two
Chewies
Collar and lead
Piddle pads
Small amount of kibble
Small dish

The First Few Days (and Nights!)

As excited as all your friends and relatives may be about your new puppy, it is better to allow the pup a few days to settle in before allowing him to "hold court." He will be in new surroundings, without the comfort and safety of his canine family for the first time, and no matter how well-adjusted he seems, there *is* physical stress involved, which is hard on the immune system, and you want to keep that to a minimum. (It is this stress that causes the mild lethargy often noticed in perfectly healthy puppies on the second day in their new homes - odds are they are simply recharging their batteries.)

You do not want to introduce a puppy during a particularly busy time for the rest of the family (the holiday season is probably the absolute worst!) and you *do* want to be sure that someone is home, nearly all the time, at least for the first few days. Remember, odds are the puppy has never been alone before and you want him to be settled in before putting him in that situation.

When arriving at home, let the puppy out briefly to eliminate, if he needs to, and then take him directly to his nursery area, bringing along the toys that are carrying the scent of home. Allow him some time to explore it before taking him out to play and sit on laps, so he will know it is "his" place. When he is out playing, leave the ex-pen door open, so, if he needs to, he can access his bathroom area. When he is ready for a nap, his "nursery" is where he should go - many pups will seek it out by themselves.

Please do not give a Havanese puppy run of the entire house - he will be nearly impossible to housebreak if you do! Think about it - giving a puppy who is maybe 5 or 6 inches tall the run of a house is like turning a toddler loose in the mall....*way* too much space to keep track of his activities! *Of all the mistakes novice owners make, this one is the most common.* Most Havanese are not reliably housebroken until 6 months or so, and slow learners can take even longer. (Any breeder who tells you this is not true most likely has puppies they are anxious to sell.) Eventually, they *will* be reliable, but the owner must be diligent, and this diligence does *not* include giving the pup the run of the house!

Even when he is not in his ex-pen, he should be confined to only a room or two where you can keep an eye on him in order to scoop him up and get him to his bathroom area in a flash if he looks like he needs to "go". If you are busy doing something else and cannot keep an eye on him, he should be in his nursery. Havanese learn best by being consistently set up to do the *right* thing, and then by being praised for it - trainers call this *positive reinforcement*. Correcting the dog *after* he has made a mistake is called *negative reinforcement*. (If it is used and sometimes, frankly, it must be, negative reinforcement needs to be administered while, or immediately after, the offense is committed - while you still have a "smoking gun", so to speak. Otherwise you will just confuse the dog.)

One of the other areas where common sense is critical right out of the gate involves introducing the Havanese puppy to other dogs. Havanese *like* other dogs - they are a sociable breed with both people and animals - and they certainly enjoy having doggy playmates. But a puppy is not fully protected against infectious diseases until he has received his entire series of puppy shots, so caution should be taken to avoid areas where many strange dogs gather, such as dog parks or even puppy classes, until that time. His

contact with other dogs should be limited strictly to those whose owners are known, whose contact with strange dogs is limited, and whose vaccinations are current.

Havanese and Kids

Unlike many Toy breeds, most Havanese enjoy the company of children. As previously mentioned, they are not well-suited to preschoolers because their small size makes them

vulnerable to inadvertent injury from toddlers, but school-age children and Havanese generally bond well together.

The first thing children need to be taught is that a puppy is a sentient being, not a plaything. They must be taught to respect the puppy's need for space and quiet time, and to understand that the puppy is essentially a baby, and needs to take naps. If the child is too young to understand that, and unable to *reliably* follow rules concerning the

puppy, it is best to wait a year or two before bringing one home. Even the best-laid plans to never allow small children to spend any time unsupervised with the puppy can go awry with heartbreaking consequences.

Children must be taught how to properly lift, hold, and carry a puppy. Havanese pups will often jump right out of your arms, or off your lap, and can injure themselves badly, so children (and adults!) must be taught to be extremely careful in that regard.

Puppies, and even adult Havanese, should *not* be allowed to play unsupervised with neighborhood children - although your own children may be well-schooled regarding small dogs, others may not be, and disasters are far better avoided than dealt with after the fact.

Canine Social Behavior...Who's Alpha here?

Despite his small size and immense charm, the Havanese, like all other breeds of domestic dogs, is descended from pack-hunting predators. Although many physical and metabolic changes occurred genetically in the dog over the years since he split off into a distinct species, all dogs still maintain the behavioral hard-wiring of a pack animal. Understanding the basics of pack behavior, therefore, is imperative to successful dog ownership.

Species with a strong social order are organized into packs and each pack is led by the Alpha animals, usually a male and a female. When this hierarchy is unchallenged, harmony reigns and the pack's survival is ensured.

Dogs coexist well with humans for two basic reasons - the first is that the dog is an adaptable fellow, and his desire to be part of a pack is so strong that he will find his position in one even if all the other pack-members are of a different species entirely. (Dogs bred to guard sheep, for instance, are traditionally raised with the flock, and come to view themselves as high-ranking members of the sheep clan, which is why they protect them.) The second reason is that man is also a pack-hunting predator, or used to be, so it's not that big of a social stretch for the dog, at least when compared to hanging out with sheep, who traditionally have occupied a considerably lower position on the food chain.

The important thing to understand is that, like man, each dog comes with the temperament for his particular pack-position pre-installed. By 7 or 8 weeks, an experienced breeder can determine the level of dominance in each pup through a series of easy tests. The more dominant pups are the ones most likely to try to jockey their way into the Alpha position. But dominance alone does not determine Alpha status in a pack - intelligence, confidence, and physical superiority are also necessary components.

In the human pack within which the domestic dog finds himself, the Alpha position(s) *must* be held by the adult humans, because even the most intelligent dogs lack the skills to ensure the pack's survival in a complex society. (The procurement of food for the pack, for instance, which is a responsibility of the Alpha members, depends more in our world on having the cash to pay the checkout girl than it does on speed, strength, and cunning, especially when obtaining the food from a supermarket, where speed, strength, and cunning in lieu of cash will most likely get you three-to-five if you are apprehended...)

Because they are small and the owner usually does not recognize what is happening, Toy breeds are often allowed to hold a much higher position in their human pack than is either desirable or practical. This, very frankly, is why so many small dogs are obnoxious. It represents the Peter Principle at its best - the dog has been promoted to a level of responsibility he cannot handle because of his physical and intellectual limitations. One does one's dog no favors to allow him to be Alpha.

When people talk about dominant dogs, they invariably use the term to describe males, but in the Havanese breed, the dominant pups in a given litter are more likely to be the females. The Havanese community is pretty much a matriarchal one.

A dominant puppy who is allowed to assert that dominance will invariably be harder to housebreak and harder to train in general. Behaviors such as play biting, growling and barking wildly at passersby out the window, and "Mexican standoffs" (where the puppy stands her ground and

The Havanese, like all dogs, is descended from pack hunting predators

barks at you after being corrected) should *not* be tolerated, as they will invariably escalate, and what is cute in a three-pound puppy is not so cute in an adult Havanese.

Although it has become politically incorrect to point this out, pack order has always been established and maintained purely by physical force, *or the implied threat thereof.* This is why an Alpha animal can modify the behavior of a pack member of lesser status with a simple steely *look* - an ability, it might be pointed out, shared by untold generations of *human* moms as well, and for exactly the same reason. As we all remember too well, what that look meant was: "Knock it off *right now* or you *will* be sorry."

If one wishes to be Alpha bitch, one must be prepared to "put one's money where one's mouth is" when faced with blatant insubordination - if you are not comfortable with that, it's best to let the breeder know you need a pup who ranks pretty low on the dominance scale, and in the Havanese breed, that is more likely to be a male.

Puppy Safety Checklist

The following things, many of which seem innocuous, can be deadly to puppies if chewed or ingested, and it is simply astounding what is attractive to them.

Houseplants- many are toxic
Electrical cords
Electrical outlets- use covers
Household cleaners
Sponges
Non-prescription pain killers
Antifreeze-keep puppies out of garage!
Cellophane
Potpourri
Sewing thread
Grapes & raisins
Chocolate

Puppy-proof your house *before* the puppy's arrival, rather than after.

To Breed ...Or Not to Breed

The issue of whether or not to breed your Havanese is something you need to understand *before* purchase, rather than after. Experienced and ethical breeders are loathe to sell breeding quality pups to rank novices, and knowing that before you start looking will frankly save you a lot of embarrassment. Many well-intentioned novices with aspirations of becoming a breeder will write letters of inquiry to breeders explaining that they would like to purchase a nice female to breed and, much to their surprise, will receive nothing but terse negative replies, assuming the inquiry is answered at all. This causes the novice to assume all breeders are a grumpy lot, who don't want anyone else competing with them for puppy sales, and they will turn to a pet shop, which will sell them a puppy bitch with full registration no questions asked. This is the worst mistake they can possibly make, but one can hardly blame them for making it..

ALL truly ethical breeders sell pups intended solely as pets to be spayed or neutered on AKC Limited registration, which means that, although the dog itself is both pedigreed and registered, its offspring are ineligible for AKC registration. Dogs with Limited registration are eligible to compete in AKC obedience and agility events, but not in conformation. Breeders do this to protect their pups from indiscriminant casual breeding, and to screen out those buyers whose intentions are less-than-honest. So the odds are the novice ,who bought from a "good" breeder, will be the proud owner of a pet Havanese on Limited registration rather than a "breeding" or "show" dog, which to an experienced breeder is one and the same.

The odds of a neophyte in the world of dogs obtaining a spectacular show-quality bitch from a top-winning breeder with full registration are slightly less than the odds of winning the Lottery and you might as well know that right out of the gate. The odds of getting a good show-quality male are slightly better, as most breeders figure the novice can do less damage with one.

Does this mean no one should even consider getting involved in breeding? Not at all. If the sport of hobby-breeding purebred dogs, which involves the showing of dogs as well, does not bring in "new blood" with every generation, it will ultimately be a footnote in history, and all purebred dogs will be produced commercially for pet shops by those whose only motive is profit, which is not in the best interest of anyone, least of all the dogs.

Breeding dogs responsibly *can* be a rewarding hobby, but it is not an inexpensive one, and there is little, if any, profit to be made. (Most good breeders are ecstatic if they break even at the end of the year and many years they do not...and that's not figuring in their time at all.) If you think it is something you might enjoy, are temperamentally suited for, and can well afford, it is best to learn as much as you can *before* you jump in with both feet. Most top breeders in *any breed* will tell you they wish they had started with more knowledge before they purchased their first "breeding-quality" dogs, the overwhelming majority of whom were not, in fact, breeding quality at all, and which cost them a lot of money, lost time, and often heartbreak.

Ideally, one should spend several years owning a Havanese, learning about the breed, and the sport of dogs in general, before attempting to breed a litter oneself. (Hence the experienced breeder's preference for selling show quality males, rather than bitches, to novices. By the time the novice has finished this first dog to his championship, he is generally quite a bit less "green", and has demonstrated a fair amount of commitment, which will make purchasing a quality bitch a good deal easier.)

The time-honored method of learning in this sport, aside from being born into it, is by having a *mentor*. Mentors are breeders of quality dogs with many years of experience behind them and, often, these breeders will work with promising newcomers, in the sport they love, passing on the wealth of knowledge they have acquired over the years to those who are sincere in their desire to learn.

How does one go about finding a mentor and, hopefully, one who will sell you a show-quality dog? The best way to start is by contacting the Havanese Club of America, the AKC Parent Club for the breed, which recognizes many local clubs throughout the country. The HCA website, www.havanese.org, maintains a list of recognized local clubs.

These local clubs welcome newcomers and sponsor events that are, in turn, competitive, educational, and social. Both new owners and "prospective" owners are generally welcome. Joining a local club and donating one's time and talents is the fastest way to learn about the breed and to get to know the Havanese breeders and owners in one's area. *Everyone* has talents that a local club can use, from organizing fundraisers, or licking stamps, to manning the trophy table at the club's specialty show.

If your area has no local Havanese club, consider joining a local All-Breed Kennel Club, whose members own all breeds of

Both new owners and "prospective" owners are generally welcome at local clubs.

dogs, as the name implies. (These clubs usually have names that denote a geographic region, with a name that always ends in "Kennel Club", such as Happy Valley Kennel Club, and they sponsor local dog shows and obedience and agility trials in that area. They often offer various classes in conformation and obedience for novices and their dogs at bargain prices. For a Kennel Club in your area, go to www.akc.org and look under "Clubs".) You will learn a lot, not the least of which is that the world of purebred dogs is smaller than it appears, and being taken under the wing of an experienced breeder of another breed is also a learning experience and often a foot in the door.

The other great place to learn about Havanese is by attending the National Specialty, a once-a year event spanning several days, which is an AKC Parent Club's version of the Kentucky Derby. Primarily a showcase for the breed's best and brightest, the National is also host to many social and educational events and one can learn more in one long weekend there than anywhere else. Information on the National is available each year on the HCA website, and reservations must be made well in advance. (Unless one is extremely self-assured, it is usually better to attend a National with someone you know, as this venue can be pretty intimidating for those fainter of heart.)

Judging the 12-18month bitch class at the 2003 National Specialty

Breeding good dogs ethically and well is a lifelong passion, full of joy and heartbreak, rewards and frustrations, and will cost you more money than you can possibly imagine. An ethical breeder is responsible for each and every dog whose existence his efforts call into being. That responsibility extends for the entire life of each dog, whom he must be prepared to take back into his home at a moment's notice should circumstances demand it. It is not an undertaking that should be considered lightly.

Plains, Trains, and Automobiles

One of the chief virtues of Havanese is their portability and it is one of the most-cited reasons for choosing the breed. Havanese are, in truth, excellent little travelers but, if you plan to take your Havanese everywhere, you need to start when they are young.

As stated earlier, this is a breed that flies easily in the passenger compartment of a plane, settling in calmly, even for extended flights, at a very young age. On the other hand, nine out of ten Havanese pups will get carsick at some time or other within the first 6 months or so, some of them with appalling regularity.

Even at this young age a Havanese pup enjoys a day at the beach.   Photo by John Decker

There are two distinct versions of Havanese carsickness- some puppies will drool incessantly in the car, soaking their faces, chests and front legs in the process. Others will merely upchuck a time or two, which in the larger scheme of things is probably preferable. The cure for both is the same- the pup must be taken for very short rides on a regular basis (somewhere besides the vet's office!) until he gets over it. This is called "desensitization" by the behavioralists and it works.

In the meantime, the droolers can be outfitted with large terrycloth baby bibs before being popped into their crate, which actually help a lot, at least to keep them drier, while the upchuckers are best placed in a crate lined with multiple layers of paper toweling, so you can remove the top layer promptly as needed. There are several herbal remedies for travel sickness worth trying that can be purchased at any health-food store - these are generally safe, and some owners have had good luck with them. Anything stronger should not be given without a veterinarian's advice.

The important thing to remember is that Havanese *will* outgrow "puppy carsickness" as long as you keep taking them for short rides in the car on a regular basis, and they are not subjected to any trauma at the end of the ride, which logically reinforces their negative feelings about the whole business. Pop them into their crate in the car cheerfully, and take them out the same way, without making much of a fuss over them one way or the other. And try to remember to take them for their little rides on an empty stomach.

Never ever leave your Hav in a parked car for any length of time - cars can turn into ovens within minutes even when the temperature outside seems mild, and even with the windows cracked. If you need to go into a store, transfer him from his crate into a soft carrier bag and take him along. Most people won't notice.

When traveling by air, you will need to purchase a soft-sided carrier that is FAA-approved, and the options here are endless. If possible, try to choose one that doesn't scream "Dog Inside", especially if you plan to take your dog into stores and restaurants that don't exactly allow them-critical if you ever plan to buy a book or eat in an airport during a layover.

You will want to make a reservation for the dog as well as yourself, for which the airlines charge a separate fee, which really makes no sense considering the dog is simply taking up space that your feet already paid for. Airlines also have limi-

All packed and ready to roll!

tations on the number of dogs allowed in the cabin per flight and, although this also makes little sense if you think about it (like what- there is only so much *oxygen* per cabin?), it is an immutable rule, so it's probably wise to make your reservations early when you are flying with your Hav.

One more caveat when flying - it is best to remove anything and everything you're wearing that might set off the alarm in the security pass-through when you have your dog along *well before you get to that point.* You will have to take the dog *out* of his carrier to send it through on the belt to be x-rayed, which means you will have him in your arms. If you set off the alarm and are pulled to the side for a full-body scan, they will not let you retrieve the carrier from the belt. Nor will they hold the dog for you, which makes sticking your arms straight out to either side while they "wand you" a real challenge.(A dog's collar and tags, for the record, *will* set off the alarm at most airports, so you need to remove that in advance as well- tuck it in the pocket of the carrier, and put it back on him when you get to the gate.)

Should this happen to you in spite of all precautions, and you find yourself in need of fortification afterwards, it is also good to know most airport bars are pretty relaxed about small dogs in carriers, especially if you don't specifically ask.

When You Can't Take Him With You

There are a few occasions where even the most travel-savvy Havanese is better left home (out-of-town funerals might be one.) In that case you will have to decide between a pet-sitter, a friend's house, or a boarding facility. The *safest* option by far is a good commercial boarding facility, but the best situation usually depends on the dog. Unless the pet-sitter will be there all the time, a Havanese left alone at home with two or three short visits from the pet-sitter per day will not be a happy camper, especially if he is young; older dogs may well prefer it, on the other hand, as it is less upsetting to their routine.

A friend's house, especially if they have a dog of their own who knows and gets along with yours, is an acceptable option provided *their entire property, especially the area outside their front door,* is secure - dogs who are boarded with friends often get it into their little heads to trek home on their own, and this scenario can cost you a friendship as well as a lost dog. Boarding kennels *assume* dogs will try to escape, and build for it.

Commercial boarding kennels, however, are a lot like breeders - they come in all varieties, and some are, frankly, awful. Get recommendations from friends and/or your vet, and visit the facility yourself *before* committing to it. Those that cater to small dogs are generally best by far, and some are downright luxurious. Beware any boarding kennel that will not let you see the area where the dogs are actually kept - *anyone* can have a nice reception area.

Be apprised that all boarding kennels will want proof of current vaccination and most require Bordetella (kennel cough) inoculation as well. If your vet does not require annual vaccinations, but rather performs titers, it is wise to inform the boarding facility of this in advance - some accept them and some do not.

Pet Action Shots

The old saying "You are what you eat" applies to Havanese as well as their owners. Proper feeding contributes to the healthy coat of this beautiful Havanese.

Chapter 5

Feeding Your Havanese

The old saying "You are what you eat" applies to Havanese as well as their owners. Health and nutrition are inexorably tied to one another, and a basic knowledge of canine nutrition, as well as the unique aspects of feeding a Havanese, will go a long way to keeping yours healthy and fit.

Understanding Canine Nutrition

In recent years, there has been a lot of interest in "natural diets" for dogs, and owners of small breeds like the Havanese seem more inclined to consider them than do owners of large breeds, or longtime experienced breeders. Although absolutely no peer-reviewed scientific research exists to support it, and scientific analysis of several of the more popular ones published in the Journal of the American Veterinary Association revealed alarming nutritional deficiencies and bacterial contamination, anecdotal evidence extolling the virtues of such diets abounds, mainly on the internet, and *never* on sites ending in *.edu.* (This, in itself, should be considered a red flag.)

In order to feed your dog right, one simple fact needs to be understood - *the domestic dog is, genetically, a "designer species" and has no wild counterpart.* Dogs are *not* the product of natural selection, but rather the product of deliberate selection by man. As such, they simply have no "natural diet", and comparing the dietary needs of a Havanese to those of a wild gray wolf is no more logical than comparing the dietary needs of a domestic Rhode Island Red hen to those of a wild ringneck pheasant.

Around eight million years ago, two of the earliest canid ancestors existed in what are now the Great Plains states - *Epicyon*, a fairly good-sized predator of the large ancestors of today's modern deer and elk, and his smaller canid cousin, *Eucyon*, who lived on much smaller prey and general scavenging. *Epicyon* followed his larger prey into extinction, while *Eucyon*, clearly a more adaptable fellow, is believed to have migrated to Asia and eventually evolved into the wolf.

Recent work in molecular genetics with maternal DNA suggests that somewhere between 135,000 and 100,000 years ago, dogs diverged genetically from the wolf, from there evolved into a separate species and, much later, into specific breeds. The predecessors of the domestic dog were the wolves who gathered around to scavenge at the campfires of early *Homo sapiens,* who appeared on the scene around the same time.

Through selection, those animals which survived and eventually evolved into the domestic dog were those who were both least threatening and best suited genetically to survive on leftover human food - *which, by that time in human history, was primarily cooked,* as early *Homo sapien* appears to be the ancestor who invented the Bar B-Q.

It was the genes of *these* animals, not those of their wilder cousins, which, over the next hundred centuries, evolved into the wide variety of breeds we have today, one of which is the Havanese. When the modern dog is compared to the wolf, differences in musculature, tendon strength, gut wall arterials and other distinct differences in the internal organs and abilities are noted. In other words, although still similar in some ways, dogs and wolves are dissimilar in many others, both physiologically and biochemically. And, for at least *one hundred thousand years*, dogs and wolves have eaten a very different diet.

The wolf is a *predatory carnivore*, but not an *obligate* one like the cat. He can live easily on small rodents, birds, less often larger prey and, when times are really tough, on worms, bugs, roots, carrion, and whatever else he can scrounge to stay alive. He eats the stomach contents, organs, muscle meat, bone, hide, feet, and hair from what he kills. Most of the carbohydrates he needs are obtained from the partially digested stomach contents of his herbivore prey because the wolf, like the dog, is monogastric (meaning he has only one stomach) and lacks the bacteria necessary to break down the cellulose wall in most raw plant-based foods. This is why feeding your dog raw veggies is pretty much a nutritional waste of time.

The domestic dog, on the other hand, is a man-made creature who's been eating human table scraps for thousands of years and, although it may seem like a good idea to feed him a natural raw diet like that of his cousin the wolf, it is not borne out by practical considerations (very little of the wolf's natural diet is available to the average suburbanite, unless one actually wishes to collect fresh road kill on a daily basis) nor by *any* nutritional studies conducted by major educational research facilities.

What the owner needs to understand about canine nutrition is that the *source* of the nutrient is far less important than the correct amount and balance of nutrients and the availability of those nutrients for the dog's use, which is referred to by nutritional scientists as "digestibility". This simple fact reflects no less than seventy years of scientific research on canine nutrition.

Digestibility of a nutrient is calculated by subtracting the amount of the nutrient found in the dog's stool from the total amount of that nutrient consumed by the same dog earlier. For example, if a dog ate 100 grams of protein and 20 grams of protein were found in the fecal material, the protein digestibility of that food source would be 80%. *This is not something the average Havanese owner can easily ascertain at home.*

This sort of research, however, *is* important. For instance, the carbohydrate digestibility in grains and other plant-based foods has actually been proven (in carefully controlled scientific studies published in peer-reviewed journals) to be significantly *increased* for domestic dogs by cooking. The digestibility of fats and proteins, on the other hand, is unaffected by cooking although, according to the USDA, the health risk to both the owner and the dog from pathogens such as E.coli, salmonella, campylobacter, and other potentially deadly bacteria and parasites found in raw meat, which cause in excess of 5,000 human deaths annually, is significantly reduced. (Dogs may indeed be less susceptible than humans to raw-meat pathogens like salmonella and E.coli, but if he passes it to you via his saliva, it doesn't matter much how susceptible *he* is, does it?)

Necessary vitamins which are affected by processing (available in a wolf's raw diet only by ingesting partially digested uncooked vegetable matter) are easily the added to a commercial mix in precise amounts scientifically determined for optimal canine health, as the dog utilizes synthetic vitamins in precisely the same manner as naturally occurring ones.

Likewise, minerals such as calcium and phosphorus can be added in the precise ratios determined to be necessary for utilization. (Improper calcium/phosphorus ratios in a dog's diet can result in skeletal abnormalities, and, like digestibility, this is not something that can be ascertained by an owner preparing a homemade diet, raw or cooked.)

In short, what the commercial dog food industry has accomplished over the past 70 or so years of canine research is to determine the nutritional requirements of the domestic dog and to make those nutrients available to the dog in the correct ratios for optimum growth and health in uniform little brown pellets that we call kibble.

No, it's not a particularly *natural food*, which some owners have a problem with, but they need to understand that *neither is* the *dog a natural animal*- he is a man-made, "designer species", and he requires a man-made, "designer food" to meet his specific nutritional requirements.

Do dogs prefer raw food? Possibly some do. But then again, most dogs like cat poop and antifreeze, too. Although the domestic dog has far greater olfactory capabilities than man, it has been recently determined that he has far fewer taste buds which should not come as a big surprise to anyone. And, much like the species who created them (and who, let's face it, will generally choose brownies over broccoli even when they know better) dogs don't always prefer what is nutritionally best for *them* either.

Making your own dog food is a little bit like rebuilding your own transmission, or representing yourself in court- you'd best be sure you *really* know what you're doing before you attempt it or the end result may be less than desirable.

Choosing the Right Food...Do Your Homework!

Dog foods, like Havanese breeders, run the gamut as far as quality goes and choosing the best one can be every bit as challenging as choosing the right breeder. If you purchase your puppy from a knowledgeable breeder, they will likely recommend the food that they themselves use, and some owners never give it much thought beyond that until someone asks them why they feed their dog that particular brand of food (subtly suggesting that doing so falls just short of outright animal cruelty) and suggests a "better" food. Their confidence shattered, and wanting the best for their Havanese, these owners will often switch to the so-called "better" (and often more expensive) food, which may, or may not, actually be better.

With a little basic knowledge, a wise owner can choose a dog food with confidence. Without it, they are at the mercy of misinformation, and there is more misinformation floating around about commercial dog foods than one can imagine - most of it on the internet.

A Regulated Industry

Stories about the big dog food companies using meat from animals that have died from awful diseases thereby causing cancer in dogs, and the inclusion of anesthetics and other weird ingredients in their foods, are internet legends that seem to take on a life of their own. One could conclude from reading some of this stuff that money-grubbing dog food companies are engaged in a conspiracy to actually make our dogs ill. A moment's rational thought should dispel some of this silliness.

Dog food companies are in business to make a profit, and their customers are without a doubt among the most demanding anywhere - the American Pet Owners who, although they may eat the most appallingly unhealthy diets themselves, will not tolerate less than perfection in what they feed their furry companions. No single industry is more concerned with consumer confidence than the pet food industry, and with good reason - one single internet rumor circulated by well-meaning but misinformed pet owners can cost them dearly, no matter how inaccurate the information being spread might be. The best argument for their success is that dogs are living longer, healthier lives than ever before, but this simple and verifiable fact often gets lost in the rhetoric.

In truth, the manufacture and distribution of dog food by the major producers in the US is well-regulated, primarily because in most cases either the food or the ingredients are shipped interstate and, as such, are subject to the same federal Food, Drug and Cosmetic Act as human foodstuffs.

"Food" is defined by this Act to mean "articles used for food or drink for man *or other animals* and articles used for components of any such article"- and this includes pet foods. The Food, Drug and Cosmetic Act is a fairly (mind-numbingly) comprehensive federal law which prohibits, among other things, the shipment of adulterated or misbranded pet foods, provides for proper clearances of drugs and food additives, and for manufacturing plant inspections.

"Misbranded" is pretty self-explanatory, but what exactly does "adulterated" mean? The adulteration section of the Act provides that "a food may be adulterated if it contains any poisonous or deleterious substances which may render it injurious to health, or if it contains any added poisonous or deleterious substance, except as provided by Food or Color Additive, Pesticide or Drug regulations; if it contains any filthy, putrid or decomposed substance; if it has been prepared, packed or held under unsanitary conditions whereby it may have been contaminated with filth or rendered injurious to health; if it contains any part or product of a diseased animal; or if its container is composed of any poisonous or deleterious substance which may render its contents injurious to health".

Whew, there's a mouthful!

A pet food may be also be considered adulterated if it is manufactured under conditions whereby it may become contaminated. The requirements for sanitation within a pet food plant are governed by the same regulations which govern human food, although there is some difference in application.

In addition to being subject to the Federal Food Drug and Cosmetic Act, dog foods are regulated by the Fair Packaging and Labeling Act, voluntary USDA inspection and regulation by the U.S. FDA, USDA and state agencies.

And all this for an animal who will cheerfully eat his own excrement and drink out of a toilet bowl, if you let him, without getting in the least bit sick.

Reading Dog Food Labels

The first step toward choosing a quality food is reading the label - in general, higher-quality dog foods will list meat or poultry as a first ingredient, although independent research has shown that dogs are perfectly capable of meeting their protein needs on a well-balanced grain-based diet. However, a grain-based food generally requires that the dog consume more volume (which in turn produces more waste) and with a breed as finicky as the Havanese, not to mention as hard to housebreak, meat or poultry-based foods have a definite edge, as you don't have to get the dog to eat as much to meet his nutritional needs.

One of the main reasons many owners are mystified by dog food choices is because they do not understand the federal labeling regulations. A dog food may look like it has thirty or more ingredients, most of them unpronounceable, and the average owner without a PhD in biochemistry is inclined to believe that some of these "chemicals" must surely be bad for the dog!

Here is a short course on how to read a dog food label:

1. By law, the products listed as part of the product name must constitute 95% of the product. Therefore, if the label says ABC Chicken and Rice, actual chicken and actual rice together must total 95% of each and every piece of kibble in the bag, and the chicken, as first listed ingredient, must comprise more than 50% but less than 97% of that. (The second ingredient must, by law, comprise at least 3%)

2. All ingredients must be listed in descending order of weight, so if the

83

first two ingredients are listed in the name of the product and comprise 95%, the other thirty are in there in *very* small amounts. (Try to break off one-*twentieth* of a piece of kibble- that's everything else.)

3. Meat meal, meat and bone meal, and poultry meal, as well as meat and poultry byproducts, which make a lot of people nervous, are produced when the rendering industry salvages various by-products including organs (and bone in the case of "meat and bone meal") from meat processing, but excluding hair, hoof, horn, feathers, and hide trimming, manure and stomach contents. The only difference between by-products and meal is rendering. *(Note: **Meat byproduct**. Any part capable of use as human food, other than meat, which has been derived from one or more cattle, sheep, swine, or goats.)* In other words, both are made from the organ parts generally consumed *as delicacies* by other cultures but not ours, except in the rural South, where people still eat things like kidneys, chitlins, scrapple, and Rocky Mountain oysters, all of which have significant nutritive value, if not wide general appeal. The hooves, hide, ears, snouts, and penises, which no one wants in their dog food, are processed separately and then sold individually to the consumer, at ridiculously high prices, for their dog's chewing pleasure. Go figure.

Both nutritive and non-nutritive additives are generally listed in dog food by their chemical names, which make them sound much scarier than they are- ascorbic acid and tocopherols, for example, sound pretty unappetizing but are simply Vitamins C and E, naturally occurring compounds used as natural preservatives. Tocopherols function as antioxidants, preventing the oxidation of fatty acids, vitamins, and some other nutrients. Taurine, which sounds like something you'd use to clean bugs and tar off your windshield, is actually an amino acid which humans synthesize in vivo but which cats and some breeds of dogs do not. (Taurine, incidentally, is classified as GRAS , or "generally recognized as safe", for cats and humans, but not dogs, as no published canine research exists on it to date.) Menadione sodium bisulfite complex, which no mere mortal can pronounce, is simply a source of Vitamin K. Surely whoever coined the phrase "don't eat it if you can't pronounce it" never considered federal labeling regulations......and is no doubt suffering from a nutritional deficiency or two by now.

The term "crude" when used in the Guaranteed Analysis on the information panel of a dog food label in the context of "crude protein" or "crude fat" refers to the total protein or fat content as determined by lab assay, rather than percentage of digestibility, which varies based on the source and processing used - it does *not* mean the protein or fat itself is somehow of low quality, like crude oil. Higher-quality dog foods generally have higher percentages of digestibility; a simple way to check is to read the "amount to feed" instructions on the bag - the higher the digestibility, the less you are advised to feed per pound of dog..

That said, the best advice when choosing a brand of dog food is to consider whether or not the company has a good reputation for nutritional research rather than simply a good marketing department and attractive packaging. There is an alarming tendency on the part of new owners to assume smaller, newer dog food companies are more "progressive", somehow, and produce a superior product. Many of these companies have both pricing and packaging that enhance this perception. They've become, in essence, the "microbreweries" of the dog food industry. But anyone can put their product in a glossy upscale bag and charge a lot for it.

The questions you, as a consumer, should be asking are:

1. **Where is the food made?**
2. **Who is responsible for day-to-day quality control?**
3. **Where is the research to support the nutritional claims?**

Larger companies will often charge less for a product of equal quality than a small company will, simply because they *can.* They maintain their own production facilities, which give them the edge, not only in pricing, but in quality control, over their smaller counterparts, who often subcontract production to independent animal feed mills, a fact of which the average consumer is generally unaware. Because the industry's "five-hundred pound gorillas" never operate below the radar of the regulatory agencies, their products rarely if ever contain ingredients that are not classified as GRAS for the species intended to consume them; a check of ingredients against the government's GRAS classifications (available online) will quickly reveal the same cannot be said for many of the smaller companies.

By and large, the bigger companies have an advantage in the "progressive" department as well. Most of them maintain extensive research facilities in which to both test their products, those currently in production and those under development, and to conduct canine nutritional research, which is a rapidly evolving field, while smaller companies have to wait until that research is published to improve their formulas.

So when choosing a dog food, do not automatically assume that the more expensive food is inherently "better" - it may be, or it may not. Just as when choosing a Havanese puppy, price should not be the sole considera-tion one way or the other.

One of the results of the canine nutritional research mentioned earlier is a recent trend toward foods that are specifically geared to the metabolic needs of different dogs. For years there was basically *puppy food* and *adult maintenance food,* although it came in many shapes and colors, and cans for those consumers who wanted a "meatier look" to what they fed their dogs. (Bear in mind that today's canned dog food is formulated pretty much the same as kibble, with water added. A *lot* of water-75-80%.) Then along came the "performance foods" with higher protein, fat and calorie counts, for hard-working dogs. On the heels of *that* addition, and just in time, came the low-calorie dog foods for sedentary, overweight couch potatoes.

The newest addition to the dog food market are foods geared toward the size of the dog which is logical, if you think about it, especially in the growth-formula foods. Small breeds like the Havanese require a proportion-ally higher caloric intake than do larger breeds, and they grow at entirely different rates. The new "small-breed formulas" designed specifically for dogs whose adult weight is less than twenty pounds now available are probably well-worth looking at when choosing a food for your Havanese. Their smaller kibble size is a plus as well, as it is designed specifically for littler mouths and teeth. They come in both growth and maintenance formulas, which also makes sense.

Once you've chosen a food for your Havanese, the issue of freshness should be given consideration. Buying your dog food at a large retail chain with a huge turnover volume generally results in a fresher product, with less chance of nutrient degradation, especially as dog food companies, in response to consumer pressure, are now relying on more natural, albeit less effective, forms of preservatives. Either way, it is wise to remember to check the "best used by" label on the bag *before* purchase.

Getting Your Havanese to Actually *Eat*...

Now, the honest truth is, no matter how much thought and research you put into choosing a high-quality food that meets the nutritional, metabolic, and individual life-stage needs of your particular Havanese, there is a fifty/fifty chance that when you get it home and put some in his dish, *he won't eat it.* Knowing this at the outset will save you a lot of time, worry, and aggravation.

As a breed, Havanese are notoriously finicky eaters. It is entirely possible that they possess more taste buds than the average dog, although this has never been scientifically researched, or it could be that the majority of them are simply not particularly interested in food. Faced with the choice between a bowl of food which they could eat, and a roll of paper towels with which they could decorate an entire room to look like Times Square on New Year's Eve, they will go for the paper towels every time.

In an effort to prevent voluntary starvation, most owners add a little fresh food to the bowl to increase palatability, and this is OK, according to most canine nutritional experts, as long as the additions do not exceed 10% of the food consumed by weight. After that point, the owner risks creating a nutritional imbalance in critical nutrients like calcium, which can result in skeletal abnormalities. It is best, therefore, to view these additions as

"Havanese condiments", whose primary purpose is to increase the odds that the little buggers will eat.

What to add? Most owners find small cut-up bits of meat, fish, or poultry, cottage cheese (bearing in mind that dogs are, by and large, pretty lactose intolerant after 6-8 weeks of age) yogurt, and occasionally veggies will entice a Havanese to consider eating. Research currently underway indicates that the Havanese breed, as a whole, may benefit from more dietary cholesterol than is generally present in commercial dog food, so the addition of whole egg (scrambled, fried, poached, boiled, and even shirred are all equally acceptable) if the dog tolerates it, or an egg yolk if he doesn't, is probably a good addition as well. As dogs have long been recognized as a "cholesterol-insensitive species"(rarely suffering from high cholesterol no matter how much they consume) and because dogs do not develop arterial plaque, the egg is a safe and healthy source of high-quality nutrition that Havanese generally find palatable. The egg's inherent natural nutritional balance is also less likely to throw off the nutritional balance of his diet than many other foods. But don't count on *any* of this working on a consistent basis.

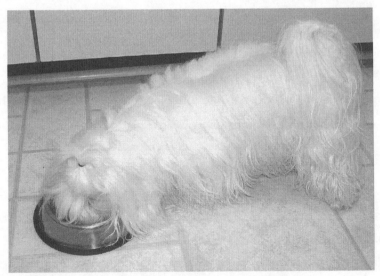

Feeding your Havanese can be a real challenge

The typical Havanese eating scenario goes something like this:

Meal One: The new owner drives across town and buys the brand of dog food suggested by the breeder, which of course the puppy has been eating all his life - let's say a high-quality chicken and rice formula for the sake of argument. The owner brings it home, and adds whatever the breeder suggests for palatability - perhaps a spoonful of cottage cheese mixed in, and some cooked egg yolk. The puppy sniffs it and recoils as though the owner is trying to *poison* him. Won't touch it. The owner, concerned that their new darling will fall over from hypoglycemia or something, offers some cut-up cooked chicken, which the puppy dutifully eats before running off to play.

Meal Two: Owner adds some cut-up chicken to the kibble along with the egg and cottage cheese. Puppy eats the chicken, the cottage cheese, and the egg, and runs off to play. Convinced the kibble is the problem, Owner drives back across town and buys the same brand in a new formula, this time lamb and rice.

Meal Three: Puppy loves the lamb and rice kibble, eats every last bit of it, but won't touch the cut up chicken, the egg, or the cottage cheese, all of which he now considers toxic waste. Puppy runs off to play.

Meal Four: Plain lamb and rice kibble? You're kidding, right? I'd like some cottage cheese, please.

Meal Five: This chicken and rice kibble isn't too bad, but you really don't expect me to eat this cottage cheesy junk, do you?

Meal Six: More eggs, please. I don't eat kibble. And what happened to that cut-up chicken, did we run out?

Meal Seven: I don't have time to eat, sorry, I have to go play now. But it was nice of you to drive across town to buy this turkey and barley kibble - too bad I don't like it. Maybe I'll like it tomorrow, though.

(This entire scenario can take place over a forty-eight- hour period, by the way.)

Playing *What Do I Want To Eat Today* is a game the average Havanese can play indefinitely, and runs a close second to *Runlikehell,* a game which seems to be firmly entrenched in the breed's genetic code. (You don't know about this? All Havanese play *Runlikehell*, which is why it actually has a name. Whether alone or in groups - for no apparent reason, they will run at lightning speed through the house, scuffing up rugs and skidding around furniture as though chased by demons, thoroughly enjoying themselves - and then it will stop as suddenly as it starts. No one knows why they do this but they all do, so you might as well be prepared.)

Unless a lamp gets knocked over, most owners find *Runlikehell* a far less annoying game than *What Do I Want To Eat Today*, which is also, apparently, firmly encoded in the Havanese DNA.

If you have no desire to play *What Do I Want to Eat Today* with your Havanese on a daily basis, you'd better make that pretty clear early on, because this breed plays to win, and it takes a steel gut to watch a small dog go three days without food (which, for the record, they *can* do without suffering any severe consequences) in the event you can't figure out exactly what it is the dog wishes you to prepare. It also makes it harder to tell when a Havanese is really not eating because he is ill, and you can waste a lot of money at the vet's trying to figure out what's wrong with a perfectly healthy finicky eater. (The answer is usually "Nothing".)

So how to you avoid it? Easy. If the puppy, who is supposed to be eating three times a day according to his breeder, refuses a meal, simply pick the food up after 15 or 20 minutes and put it in the fridge. Offer it to him at the next scheduled mealtime without altering it one iota. Usually by that time the puppy will actually be hungry, and you will have won. (Round one, anyway. They *really* want to play this game, so they will keep trying to get you to play too. You must stand firm. One slip-up and you've had it.)

The reason this works with no damage to the puppy is because the breeder, who has been feeding the whole litter of puppies three times a day and instructs you to do likewise, probably suspects that each puppy is actually only eating *twice* a day, but doesn't know (or care, if it's an experienced Havanese breeder) which ones are really eating at which meals, and it changes daily anyway. In fact, the breeder is probably *immune* to it because odds are, like many others, they feed their adult dogs twice a day, although each dog only eats once, sometimes in the morning, sometimes in the evening, depending on how each individual is feeling about it that day. They simply pick the dishes up after 15 or 20 minutes and try again at the next mealtime. Some breeders and owners give up and only feed their dogs once a day, but if the dog isn't hungry at that particular moment, he'll then go *48 hours* without eating if you try to stay on schedule, and this bothers a lot of people too much to try it.

Now, you *can* allow your Havanese free choice food, which is called "ad lib feeding" in canine nutrition studies, but this is a bad idea for several reasons. The first has to do with food spoilage - if the dog is on an ad lib system, you are really locked into dry kibble for reasons of bacterial contamination, and most Havanese will get pretty bored with that in a hurry. The second is that an ad lib fed Havanese will turn into a "grazer", and take his food, one piece at a time, out of his bowl to someplace comfortable like the couch, eat that piece, and then go back for one more, repeating the process ad infinitum. (I am not making this up!) This gets frankly annoying after a while. The third is the simplest and most important- he who controls the food in any pack is the Alpha, and if that's not *you*, you're in trouble on a lot of levels.

Now if this all sounds insane to you, that's because it is. But it is also a reality of Havanese ownership, unless you are lucky enough to accidentally obtain one of the 1.5 % of the breed who are reliably good eaters. If you honestly want a dog who will eat whatever is put into his bowl at mealtime without fail, and without all this fooling around, my advice to you is to get a Pug. It's their strong suit.

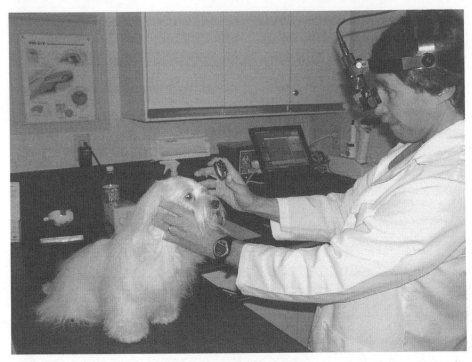

Health testing is critical to the well-being of the Havanese breed. Above, the CERF exam which should be done annually on all Havanese, at least until age 8.
Below, the BAER test to evaluate hearing...this painless test can be done on pups as young as 6 weeks and only needs to be done once.

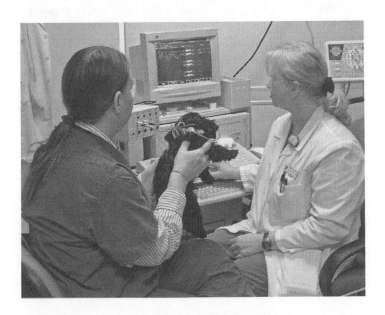

Chapter 6

Havanese Health...the Unvarnished Truth

Someone once famously suggested that if one wished to live a long and healthy life, the best thing one could do to ensure it was to make certain one had PARENTS who'd lived long and healthy lives. The same is true of dogs. Good nutrition and the practice of skilled veterinary medicine, both of which have come a long way over the years, can still only do so much, no matter how committed the owner or skilled his vet. The surest way to keep a dog healthy, sound, and long-lived is to buy him from *certified* healthy, sound, and long-lived bloodlines to begin with.

Questions about health are among the most important ones you can ask and you need to be asking most of them of the breeders *before*, rather than your veterinarian *after*, you buy a Havanese.

Beware of the breeder who tells you that the Havanese is "a healthy breed with few, if any, genetic problems" *because it is simply untrue.* Havanese, like most purebreds, *do* have genetic problems, some of which are lethal or life-threatening. Others are painful to the dog and expensive surgery may be required so that quality of life can be maintained. Sugar-coating this fact in order to sell puppies is not in *anyone's* best interest, least of all that of the breed itself.

Starting Out Healthy...and Wise

The single most important thing you, as an owner, can do to ensure your Havanese lives a long and healthy life is to purchase your puppy from a breeder who is aware of the health concerns in the breed in the first place. Breeders who are both educated and realistic about genetic and congenital problems in their breed are far less likely to produce them and far *more* likely to stand behind the puppy should they occur despite their best efforts.

Breeders who do little, or no, health-screening before breeding two dogs together because they "have no problems in their lines" should be avoided at all cost. One might intelligently wonder how they have arrived at this conclusion without the benefit of modern veterinary technology! Without an x-ray, it's pretty hard to tell if a dog suffers from hip dysplasia and a dog can develop cataracts *years* before he starts actually running into walls. And it is a truly rare and gifted breeder who can detect a mitral valve insufficiency in a dog by casual observation.

These same breeders, when faced with a puppy buyer whose well-loved pet now requires expensive and painful surgery to correct a problem that they've "never had in their line", are the most likely to argue that "there is no proof that it is hereditary" and to refuse to honor their guarantee against genetic defects. And, sadly, from their extremely limited perspective this argument actually makes sense to them.

The best way to avoid having to deal with this sort of twisted logic is to purchase from a breeder who health-screens in the first place. If it means you have to wait a little longer, and if it costs you a few dollars more, you may rest assured it will be the best time and money you have ever spent.

Good Havanese breeders understand that the breed's health problems cannot be ignored, and they make no effort to "sweep them under the rug". The simple truth is this: *most* health problems in any breed (and in man as well, for that matter) are the result of simple mutations in specific genes. That is, in the normal, or "wild type" case, such *genes do not cause disease.* Rather, it is only when some change in the sequence of the gene occurs that disease MAY result.

Although we often hear about "the cancer gene", or "the cataract gene", these terms are both misleading and scientifically incorrect. Genes contain the "recipes" for various chemical processes in the body critical to life. It is when a gene mutates spontaneously, and its particular recipe for producing a protein is altered, that "disease" can result. These gene *mutations,* or alleles, will continue to be passed on from one generation to the next, spreading their "altered recipes" insidiously among a breed's population until they are everywhere and the health of the entire breed is compromised. *Genetic mutations will generally not disappear on their own*. Halting their spread in any breed, and with any genetic disease, requires a two-pronged approach:

1. Breeders must *identify* the genetic problems in a breed, create a climate in which admitting one has produced an affected animal comes without penalty, so that the actual prevalence of the problem within the breed can be ascertained, and then applying the best classical animal husbandry practices they can to avoid the further spread of these problems, given the knowledge currently available to them, without sacrificing essential breed type, soundness, or temperament, until a causative gene can be identified.

2. Breeders and pet owners alike must support research into the molecular genetics of the disease, both financially and by sharing pedigree information and providing DNA, when needed, from affected animals. In this way, the precise genetic mutation may be first identified and then systematically and painlessly removed from the gene pool through simple genetic testing. This 21st century solution, which is neither inexpensive nor easy to effect, is the *only* way to assure the healthy future of a breed without sacrificing the progress that breeders have achieved through years of hard work. It was *unimaginable* a mere decade or two ago.

Those who care about this breed, both pet owners and breeders alike, have risen to meet the challenge admirably, in a few short years, and the future of the Havanese breed is indeed brighter because of it. H.E.A.R.T., the Havanese breed's independent non-profit Health Foundation, through the generosity of its individual donors, the Havanese Club of America, and the AKC Canine Health Foundation has, since its inception in 1999, supported breed-specific research projects that may well result in the eradication of many of the

breed's most serious health issues in the foreseeable future. It is in support of this effort that all the profits from this book are being donated to the current H.E.A.R.T. research project until the grant total is reached.

Ockham Syndrome, or "OS"

The research project that H.E.A.R.T. is currently supporting, at Texas A&M University, is geared toward identifying the gene mutation(s) responsible for a collection of disorders reported with some frequency in Havanese and collectively referred to as Ockham Syndrome, or OS.

A *syndrome*, by medical definition, is a collection of symptoms, either congenital or developmental, which occur together and usually have a single underlying genetic cause. (In humans, Down's syndrome, caused by a single chromosomal abnormality, is probably the best-known.) The "symptoms" collectively referred to as Ockham Syndrome in the Havanese breed are disorders which affect various systems in the body and so have, logically, always been presumed unrelated. They may appear singly, but more often appear in combination, and the degree of severity of each is variable, ranging from mild to life-threatening.

These symptoms are briefly described below.

(The Health Committee of the Havanese Club of America conducted a world-wide anonymous online health survey of the breed in 2004, and received health data on 756 Havanese, representing a statistically significant cross-section of the population. Where applicable, the rate of occurrence for each symptom as reported by owners in the survey has been included.)

Chondrodysplasia and other skeletal abnormalities

(Chondrodysplasia was reported in an astounding 1 out of every 5 Havanese... In 1 out of every 36 Havanese, surgery was performed to repair orthopedic problems.)

Many breeders assume that CD is a *disease* in Havanese, and confuse it with Ockham Syndrome. In reality, chondrodysplasia in Havanese is a *condition* and this condition may be a *symptom* of an underlying disease. For the purposes of the research currently underway, it is important to understand that CD is considered to be one of many symptoms of OS.

One of the clear patterns that has emerged from all the research accomplished to date is that the healthiest Havanese are also the most physically sound animals. This is not coincidental.

The Havanese Standard has *always* called for a dog with well-boned, straight forelegs, with feet that turn neither in nor out. The distance from the withers to the elbow should equal the distance from the elbow to the ground. Unfortunately, as with any heavily-coated breed, this is not easy to see in a Havanese, and many dogs have short, bowed, twisted, or asymmetric legs beneath their pretty coats, with one or both forefeet turning out at the pasterns. Traditionally referred to as a "fiddle front", these skeletal abnormalities are caused by uneven and/or premature closure of the growth plates of the long bones, and/or suppression of the growth of the long bones themselves. The forelegs are usually affected to a greater degree than the hind legs.

This condition of premature growth plate closure is characterized by various skeletal abnormalities and considered the norm in dwarf breeds. It is

This dog is chondrodysplastic- note the short legs and large head.

variously referred to by veterinary orthopedic specialists as achondroplasia, chondrodystrophy, or *chondrodysplasia,* ("CD"). All mean precisely the same thing - abnormal development of bone from cartilage.

Chondrodysplasia can be a mild condition, with slight bowing or simply short legs, causing no discomfort to the animal, or it can be severe, in which case extensive orthopedic surgery may be needed to both alleviate pain and allow the Havanese to function normally. This surgery, most frequently an ulnar or radial/ulnar osteotomy, is generally performed at around a year of age, when bone growth is nearly complete, and surgical success is variable.

The Missing Link..... Cholesterol

Although not all CD dogs overtly display any other health problems, it is significant that most of the serious, and/or life-threatening, health problems such as cleft palate, liver and kidney defects, major cardiac defects, seizures, and cataracts, have been identified in Havanese who *also* display symptoms of chondrodysplasia, or the offspring of these dogs.

These defects have been linked to an inborn error in the biosynthesis of cholesterol in humans and other mammals, and research at Texas A&M University, under the direction of Keith Murphy PhD, is underway to determine whether this is the cause in Havanese as well. Many malformation syndromes, all sharing a commonality of skeletal dysplasia, have been extensively studied in man in recent years, and individual causative gene mutations in cholesterol biosynthesis have been identified in at least a dozen.[1]

The most common, and well-studied, of these in humans is a disease called Smith-Lemli-Opitz Syndrome, which causes symptoms identical to those seen in affected Havanese. The cause of SLOS is a group of mutations in one gene necessary for the production of a single enzyme critical to the last step in normal cholesterol biosynthesis. The fact that mutation of **one gene** *necessary for cholesterol synthesis can produce symptoms as varied as cataracts, renal dysplasia, cleft palates, cryptorchidism, and hearing loss is simply mind-boggling to most of us, but we may as well get used* *to it - 21st century molecular genetics no doubt has many more such surprises in store for us!*

It is important to understand that although an *excess* of cholesterol in the bloodstream is considered undesirable, cholesterol and its precursor sterols are essential for many cellular and developmental processes in the body. An *insufficiency* of cholesterol can be deleterious and even life-threatening, especially during gestation, where it can result in birth defects.[2] One reason for this involves a family of "signaling" genes known as the *hedgehog family.* (I swear I am not making this up!)

Hedgehogs????? Surely you jest.....

Many of the developmental malformations in these syndromes occur In tissues and structures whose embryonic patterning depends on signaling by the hedgehog family of secreted proteins. Decreasing levels of cellular sterols (the "building blocks" of cholesterol) correlate with diminished response to the hedgehog signal.[3] Depending upon the target tissue of the particular hedgehog gene, this disruption in hedgehog signaling can result in malformation of neural tube development, limbs, various organs including the heart, liver, and kidneys, the nervous system, the gastrointestinal system, as well as the eyes, ears, skin, teeth, male reproductive organs, and hair which, admittedly, does not leave much of the dog unaffected. Three hedgehog genes have been identified to date: Sonic hedgehog (*Shh*), which affects basic cell differentiation and right/left symmetry, has been identified in nearly every tissue in the body; Indian hedgehog (*Ihh*), which affects bone growth; and Desert hedgehog (*Dhh*), which affects male gonadal development. And, yes, Sonic hedgehog, which is characterized by its spiky appearance under an electron microscope, was indeed named for the computer game character of the same name...molecular geneticists tend to be both brilliant and young , which also explains why there is a gene which affects the ability to metabolize alcohol named (I swear I am NOT making this up!) Cheap Date.

Back to Chondrodysplasia....

Unlike most of the other disorders associated with errors in cholesterol biosynthesis, abnormalities in skeletal structure (termed *chondrodysplasia* in this breed) can be easily ascertained by any owner with the aid of a bottle of shampoo, a camera, and a copy of the Havanese Standard in hand. Breeders refer to this as "soaping" a dog, and those who are aware of the direction of the current health research do it as a matter of course on both breeding dogs and puppies.

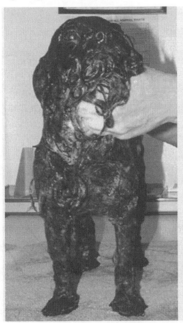

The dog on the left has normal skeletal structure. The dog on the right is chondrodysplastic, with abnormally short legs and asymmetric bowing of the left foreleg. She also has cataracts and mitral valve insufficiency. OS dogs often display multiple symptoms.

Slathering a damp (but not dripping) Havanese with thick shampoo, standing him on a towel-covered table and having an assistant take 3 photographs - from the front, the right and the left side - will generally reveal any bowing, twisting, abnormal shortness of the legs, or asymmetry, where one leg is significantly longer (and usually more bowed) than the other and the elbows are at different heights in relation to the ribcage. All of these are *skeletal abnormalities* in this breed.

In general, length of leg can be ascertained by comparing the distance from the withers to the elbow (in other words the depth of the ribcage) with the distance from the elbow to the floor - in a dog whose growth plates have closed normally, and whose elbows reach the chest (rather than being half-way up the ribcage, which indicates an abnormally short humerus), this distance is roughly equal, and the bones of the foreleg should appear straight when viewed from both the front and the side. Significantly shorter legs indicate premature closure of the growth plates, which is also a symptom of OS.

Should the owner suspect anything amiss when looking at the resulting photographs, a radiograph of the front legs, by a clinical or orthopedic vet , will generally confirm or alleviate the suspicion of chondrodysplasia.

An increasing number of Havanese breeders soap their dogs prior to making breeding decisions, which is prudent, and many will provide soaped photographs of the parents upon request. Those breeders who are unaware of the existence of chondrodysplasia, much less Ockham Syndrome, are clearly not in a position to avoid perpetuating it in the puppies they sell, and the buyer is incurring significant risk by purchasing from them.

Although premature closure of the growth plates is caused by disruption in the Indian hedgehog gene due to reduced cholesterol synthesis,[4] the precise mode of inheritance for OS itself is at this point unknown. However, the basic tenets of good animal husbandry suggest that breeding two chondro-dysplastic Havanese together would be unlikely to produce a high percentage of offspring that were an improvement over either parent in this regard.

Other Orthopedic Problems

Also associated with OS in this breed are *syndactyly, patellar luxation, elbow dysplasia,* and *Legg-Calve-Perthes.*

Syndactyly is a congenital skeletal abnormality commonly associated with certain diseases of cholesterol biosynthesis in which the bones of the toes are fused[7]. The condition may be so severe as to affect the dog's ability to walk normally, or it may be very subtle and go unnoticed by the owner.

Patellar luxation is a condition in which the patella, which normally rides in a groove at the distal end of the femur is unstable, and luxates, or slips, out of place. This condition, long understood to have an underlying genetic basis, is often the result of "uneven wear" on the femur caused by skeletal abnormalities, especially in adult dogs of this breed. The severity of the luxation is designated by grades, with Grade 1 being the mildest and Grade 5 the most severe. Generally, grades 3-5 require surgical correction.

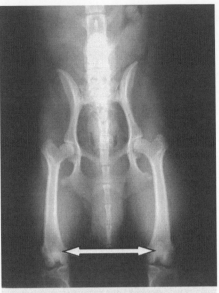

Normal Havanese Hips
Note patellas in normal position

Elbow dysplasia refers simply to abnormality of the elbow joint, which often lead to degenerative joint disease, and may require surgical repair. It is often associated with bowed, chondrodysplastic forelegs in this breed.

Legg-Calve-Perthes is the name given to necrosis of the femoral head, caused by vascular interruption. It generally appears before a year of age, and causes pain that results in apparent lameness of one hind leg. Too often attributed to injury, LCP is known to have a genetic basis and is not uncommon in dogs with other symptoms of OS. Treatment for LCP generally involves surgical removal of the femoral head and neck, after which an "artificial joint" forms, allowing the dog to function with a degree of normalcy.

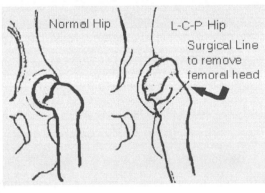

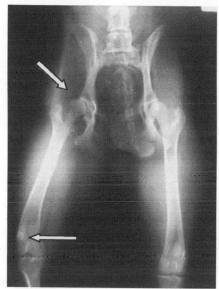

Canine Hip Dysplasia is a condition that exists in many breeds, including the Havanese. Believed to be a polygenic disorder, hip dysplasia simply means "badly formed" hips - it does *not* mean the hips are "displaced". Hip dysplasia results in degenerative joint disease for the dog, but does *not* always cause limping immediately, especially in young animals. Severe hip dysplasia often requires corrective surgery and can cause significant pain for the dog. At this time it is unknown whether or not CHD is related to cholesterol biosynthesis, but good breeding practices dictate that all dogs should be screened for it prior to breed-

Dysplastic hips—note shallow acetabulum and flattened femoral head on right hip . The patella is also abnormally positioned.

ing. This can *only* be ascertained by radiograph. (Many vets *do not* require that a Havanese be sedated in order to x-ray their hips - it pays to ask around.)

Heart and liver disorders

(1 out of every 20 Havanese were reported to have liver abnormalities. The Veterinary Medical Database ranks Havanese #1, by percentage, among all breeds in occurrence of liver shunts.)

(1 out of every 20 Havanese were also reported to have heart abnormalities.)

Congenital abnormalities in the major organs, including the heart and liver, are associated with a disruption in the signaling pathway of the Sonic Hedgehog gene during embryological development[5], and are fairly common symptoms of OS in Havanese. These defects can range from mild to lethal, and *all* Havanese, not only breeding dogs, should ideally be screened for them.

Heart defects seen in Havanese include the most severe congenital anomalies, such as **atrial and ventricular septal defects**, which are often lethal in puppies, as well as milder, less life-threatening **mitral valve insufficiencies**, which may occur later. Auscultation by one's clinical vet will usually reveal a heart murmur. (This is a process during which one listens to the heart with a stethoscope, in case you were wondering....) If a murmur is detected, it is wise to seek the services of a veterinary cardiac specialist to see if treatment is warranted.

Hepatic (Liver) dysfunction in this breed, as is the case with most of the other problems, can range from a potentially lethal portosystemic shunt, to severe hepatic microvascular dysplasia, to abnormally high ALT and/or bile acid assays. **Portosystemic shunt** is a congenital abnormality in which the blood, which is normally filtered of toxins as it passes through the liver, is shunted around it. Untreated, a PSS may be ultimately fatal, as the systems become toxic. Single, extrahepatic shunts are most likely to be successfully repaired surgically, while multiple, intrahepatic shunts are usually inoperable, and the prognosis for survival is poor. **Hepatic microvascular dysplasia** is a congenital condition that generally presents with the same symptoms as a PSS, but diagnostic tests fail to reveal a shunt and, often, multiple biopsies are required before the characteristic lesions are revealed. Unlike an extrahepatic shunt, treatment is mostly supportive because surgical repair is impossible, and the prognosis for long-term survival is less than wonderful.

Abnormally high post-prandial bile acid levels in the bloodstream are generally an indicator of liver dysfunction. Bile acids, one of the end products of cholesterol biosynthesis, are produced in the liver and stored in the gall bladder for release during the digestive process, where they are necessary for the absorption of fatty acids and the four fat-soluble vitamins (A, D, E. and K). These bile acids are typically re-circulated *back* into the *hepatocytes*, or cells of the liver, post-prandially (after eating), with very little escaping into the systemic blood. "Sick" hepatocytes are incapable of this re-uptake, which is why high levels of bile acids in the bloodstream indicate liver dysfunction.[6] Many Havanese with abnormally high bile acids appear overtly healthy, but no long-term studies exist in this area.

Urogenital Disorders

(1 out of every 19 Havanese reported urinary tract problems.)

(1 out of every 16 Havanese males were reported to be cryptorchid.)

Reported less frequently in Havanese, but not uncommon, is **renal (kidney) dysplasia**, a congenital anomaly common in children suffering from diseases of cholesterol biosynthesis, with an incidence rate there of 40%.[7] Renal dysplasia should be suspected when growth is significantly below the norm, and can be confirmed through diagnostic testing. Kidney dysplasia is not repairable, and treatment is primarily supportive, with variable prognosis.

Bladder problems, including bladder infections, crystals in the urine, and bladder stones, on the other hand, are much more common in Havanese and generally respond well to treatment.

Pseudohermaphroditism and other forms of ambiguous genitalia have been reported, and **cryptorchidism** (failure of a testicle to descend into the scrotum) is fairly common in the breed. Like ambiguous genitalia, cryptorchidism is attributed to a disruption in the signaling pathway of *Dhh* (the Desert Hedgehog gene),[3] but it is a mild symptom at best. Cryptorchid dogs are ideally neutered and placed in pet homes, in which they make wonderful companions and usually display no other overt symptoms of OS.

HPE

(48% of the Havanese producing offspring reported at least one major anomaly related to Shh disruption in those offspring, including skull abnormalities (2), cleft palate (5) open fontanel (8) and missing incisors (25) 1 out of every 4 litters included stillborn pups or neonatal mortality.)

HPE is short for the virtually unpronounceable *holoprosencephaly*, which represents the partial or complete failure of the neural tube (the earliest structure to form during embryogenesis and the basis for the axial skeleton on any vertebrate) to divide into right and left lobes. It is also caused by disruption in the signaling pathway (or in rare cases by a mutation) of *Shh* , which is responsible for right/left symmetry in the body.[3] Complete failure, of course, is inconsistent with life, and will result in spontaneous abortion, resorption of the fetus, or stillbirth. Partial failure will result in major skull defects, the most severe being **incompletely developed skull, cyclopia,** and **cleft palates.** Less severe symptoms include **open fontanels, microphthalmia, and micrognathia** (underdeveloped lower jaw, or "parrot-mouth"). The mildest symptom of HPE is **single maxillary central incisor,**[9] which is both fairly benign and not uncommon in this breed.

Ocular Disorders

(1 out of every 7 Havanese were reported to have ocular abnormalities.)

(1 out of every 10 Havanese, according to 2003 CERF data (1,114 dogs examined) were reported to have either cataracts of any size or lens luxation)

The most common ocular disease in Havanese, by far, is **cataracts.** Defined as an opacity of the normally crystalline lens, a cataract forms when

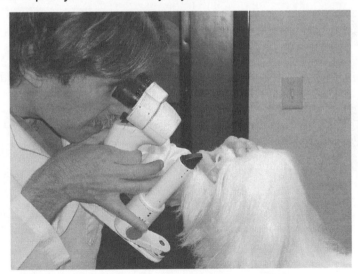

Evaluating eyes with slit lamp during CERF examination.

the biochemical mechanisms of lens metabolism fail and electrolyte, lipid, and glucose metabolic pathways are affected. Increased hydration results in formation of vacuoles and water clefts. Lens fibers undergo oxidative damage which results in retention of Na (sodium) and Ca (calcium), and eventually the entire lens opacifies. [10]

106

When the cataract has progressed to the point that it is vision-impairing, it will generally be visible to the naked eye, but incipient (punctate) cataracts can best be diagnosed by a veterinary ophthalmologist using an indirect ophthalmoscope and slit-lamp; *a superficial exam by your regular veterinarian is very unlikely to detect early cataracts!* It is strongly recommended that every Havanese, even those not intended for breeding, be checked annually by an ACVO-certified veterinary ophthalmologist for its own well-being. Rapidly progressing cataracts can lead to secondary glaucoma which, if left untreated, may require surgical removal of the entire eye. Cataract surgery is usually more successful when done early rather than late.

Other eye problems seen in Havanese include **retinal dysplasia, luxation of the lens**, and **vitreous** and **retinal degeneration**. To date, all reported cases of blindness in Havanese have been in dogs also displaying skeletal abnormalities. As the cells of the eye normally contain more cholesterol than any other cells in the body, it is not surprising that ocular disorders (primarily cataracts, where the incidence rate is around 10%) are common in diseases of cholesterol biosynthesis[11]. They are considered to be a symptom of OS in this breed.

Deafness and other neurological disorders

(1 out of every 42 Havanese were reported to have neurological disorders, excluding behavior)

(1 out of every 62 Havanese reported partial or total deafness.)

The nervous system is another that is regulated by hedgehog signaling and disruptions in these targeted tissues can result in several seemingly unrelated disorders. The role of cholesterol metabolism and resultant impaired *Shh* function in brain development has been the focus of much research attention in recent years.[12] Surely the worst are **seizures** for which, unfortunately, there are no screening tests.

Behavioral abnormalities are common in children with diseases of cholesterol abnormalities, as is **cognitive deficit**.[13] OS should be suspected here in Havanese when all other avenues have been explored, but it is important to differentiate between dominant behavior that is environmentally triggered (usually as a result of a puppy being allowed to jockey for a higher pack position than is appropriate) and idiopathic aggression, which is *not* normal in the breed. Mental retardation and autism have also been reported in the breed, although rarely, most likely because they are pretty hard to measure in a dog.

Far less devastating is **unilateral deafness** and, with lesser frequency, **bilateral deafness** both of which occur with unknown frequency in the Havanese breed. The *reason* that the frequency is unknown is because unilateral deafness, caused by cochlear nerve dysfunction, can only be ascertained by means of a BAER test. This test, which is painless, non-invasive, and takes about five minutes, measures brain wave response to a series of clicks transmitted through soft earplugs inserted into the ears, and measured by means of a series of fine electrodes, which are slipped painlessly under the skin on specific parts of the skull.

It is impossible to for an owner, or even his vet, to diagnose unilateral deafness in a Havanese, as they appear entirely normal. A unilaterally deaf Havanese can hear the refrigerator door open when sound asleep in the next room, so it is unwise to consider it a reliable test of normal hearing, although many breeders apparently do. Until such time as all breeders are willing to spend the time and money to BAER test, the incidence of deafness in the breed will be impossible to accurately assess.

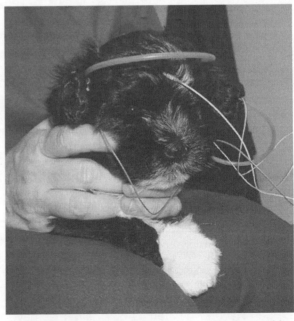

BAER testing is painless and well tolerated by Havanese

As cochlear nerve deafness is caused by disruption in *Shh*[14] knowledgeable breeders BAER test both their breeding stock, to avoid inadvertently breeding two unilaterally deaf dogs together, *and* their puppies, to avoid inadvertently adding them to the gene pool. Unilaterally deaf puppies, like cryptorchids, usually display no other overt symptoms, make fine pets, and are generally sold for standard pet price. Unfortunately, a fair number of them are also probably sold as show/breeding dogs by breeders who do not bother to BAER test.

Gastrointestinal Disorders

(1 out of every 11 Havanese were reported to have had GI problems)

Both foregut and hindgut development are regulated by *Shh*[15], and malformations here range from extreme, such as **imperforate anus**, which is exactly what it sounds like and is considered to be a lethal defect in dogs, to **malabsorption syndrome**, to less life-threatening conditions such as **inflammatory bowel syndrome**, or a simply **"oversensitive" digestive tract**, which is not uncommon at all. (Malformations of foregut development can also result in both **tracheal stenosis** and **tracheal collapse**)

Coat and Skin Disorders

(1 out of every 9 Havanese reported skin problems)
(1 out of every 22 Havanese reporting offspring produced shorthaired pups)

Diseases of cholesterol biosynthesis are often associated with abnormalities of the skin and hair as both the growth cycle of the hair follicle itself and the sebaceous gland that produces sebum, which is both a lubricant and bacteriostatic, are regulated by Shh expression.[16,17] For this reason, both **sebaceous adenitis** and **the shorthaired phenotype** (which is *not* a health problem per se) are considered to be symptoms of OS in this breed.

Immune System Disorders

(1 out of every 11 Havanese reported allergies)
(1 out of every 6 Havanese reported ear infections)

Otits media and externa (ear infections) are commonly associated with errors in cholesterol biosynthesis[18], and the same appears to be true in Havanese as well. There are two possibilities here - one is a fundamental abnormality in immune function, which would explain the relatively high incidence of **allergies** also reported, and the other is a congenitally small ear canal, which has been noted in both affected children *and* Havanese, and which would predispose the ear to infection.

Symptoms of Ockham Syndrome

Skull defects
(cleft palate, open fontanel, micrognathia)

Organ defects
(heart, liver kidney defects)

Skeletal abnormalities
(CD, skeletal asymmetry, patellar luxation, LCP)

Intestinal abnormalities
(imperforate anus, malabsorption, inflammatory bowel syndrome)

Ocular abnormalities
(microphthalmia, cataracts, retinal abnormalities)

Gondal abnormalities
(pseudohermaphroditism, cryptorchidism)

Deafness
(unilateral and bilateral)

Coat and skin abnormalities
(sebaceous adenitis, shorthaired phenotype)

Missing Incisors
(single central maxillary incisor)

Minimizing Risk

Life, unfortunately, does not come with guarantees. Because the genetics behind them are not yet well-understood, the health problems described above can and do occur in spite of a breeder's best efforts, and sometimes the results are heartbreaking for the owner. But a responsible breeder will do everything they can to minimize the risk of this happening, and risk is *significantly* minimized by complete health-screening and honestly evaluating for skeletal abnormalities *before* breeding two animals together, to maximize the chances of producing healthy puppies.

Likewise, longevity is hereditary. A puppy whose grandparents and great-grandparents are sound and healthy at 10 or even 15 years of age is much more likely to arrive there himself than one whose ancestors died young. Beware the breeder who knows little or nothing about the pup's extended family. A wise buyer, understanding that a breeder is under no obligation to volunteer information that is not requested, will specifically ask about the grandparents, older siblings, and other close relatives as well.

Havanese Health Screening 101

One could perhaps assume from the previous litany of maladies that the Havanese is one of the unhealthiest breeds around, but that is simply not the case.

None of the health problems seen in the breed are unique to Havanese; the stewards of this breed (breeders and pet owners alike) have simply taken a pro-active approach to solving the health problems that do exist by both reporting them (which many breeds do not), and by attempting to find the underlying cause and the gene(s) responsible. Until this is accomplished, though, what can concerned and ethical breeders do to minimize the risks of producing unhealthy dogs?

They can do what experienced breeders have *always* done - apply the principles of good animal husbandry practices.

The most basic of these is that one never knowingly breeds two animals together who display the same "fault" because, *regardless of that fault's particular mode of inheritance,* the larger percentage of the offspring from such a pairing are unlikely to represent an improvement on the parents.

In the Havanese breed, the *only* way to make sure you are not pairing two animals with the same health problem together is to health-screen, and *there is no valid excuse* for a breeder not health-screening their breeding stock, *and* registering the results of such screening with OFA. All the health-screening recommended for Havanese is painless, non-invasive, inexpensive when compared to the price of a single puppy sold, and can be performed without anesthesia.

The results of the eye exam must be sent to the Canine Eye Registry Foundation at Purdue University in order to be granted a CERF number. BAER test, Hip films and Patellar certification are sent to the Orthopedic Foundation for Animals to be recorded in their CHIC (Canine Health Information Center) database, which also cross-lists with CERF.

Havanese which have had all four tests recorded by OFA are granted a CHIC number. This certification may be verified online by accessing the CHIC database at www.offa.org and simply entering the dog's registered name into the "search" box on their home page. This registry is open to pets as well as show and breeding dogs, and pet owners can contribute meaningfully to the future of the breed by having their dogs certified by OFA and added to the database.

Basic health tests recommended for the Havanese

- Annual eye exam performed by an ACVO-certified ophthalmologist to screen for eye disease
- A one-time BAER (brain auditory evoked response) test to screen for congenital deafness
- A hip x-ray to screen for canine hip dysplasia at two years of age
- A veterinary exam to screen for patellar luxation at one year of age
- A blood chem. panel including bile acid assays to screen for liver and kidney dysfunction.

Because the Havanese has an alarmingly high incidence of liver shunts (according to the Veterinary Medical Database maintained by Purdue University, the Havanese currently ranks #1 in rate of occurrence for liver shunts among all AKC breeds) and because renal dysplasia is also being d in the breed, it is recommended that breeders also screen their breeding stock for both hepatic and renal dysfunction by means of a simple blood test, referred to as a *Liver Panel,* (an SA 320 if done by Antech Labs.) The panel includes a Complete Blood Count (CBC), Chemistry Panel (which includes measurement of hepatic and renal function) and paired bile acids. Breeders should also screen for heart defects by cardiac exam which, given the incidence of heart defects in the breed, is wise.

References:

[1]Kelley, R.I. Inborn errors of cholesterol biosynthesis. *Adv Pediatr.* 2000; **47**:1-53

[2] Report NHLBI Working Group on the Role of Cholesterol and Lipids in Embryonic Development and Congenital Disease. 1998, *Vanderbilt University, Nashville, TN*

[3]Cooper, Michael K. et al. 2003 A Defective Response to Hedgehog Signaling in Disorders of Cholesterol Biosynthesis. *Nature Genetics.* 33 online Mar 2003; doi:10.1038/ng1134

[4]Wu, Shufang, De Lucca, F. 2004 Role of Cholesterol in the Regulation of Growth Plate Chondrogenesis and Longitudinal Bone Growth. *J. Biol. Chem.***279**: 4642-4647

[5]Heussler, H S, Suri, M. Sonic Hedgehog. Implications For Human Development *Molec. Path.* 2003; **56**:129-131

[6] Secretion of Bile and the Role of Bile Acids in Digestion. *Pathophysiology of the Digestive System.* 1998, *Colorado State University*

[7]Multiple Congenital Anomaly/Mental Retardation Syndromes. NLM. *NIH publication.*

[9] Roessler,E, Belloni E, Gaudenz K, et al. Mutations in the C-terminal domain of Sonic Hedgehog cause holoprocencephaly. *Hum Mol. Genet* 1997; 11;1847-1853

[10]Ramsey, David T DVM, Diplomate ACVO. Text. Current Topics in Ophthalmology. 2000*Publication: Richmond Academy of Veterinary Medicine.*

[11] Herman Gail E. Disorders of cholesterol biosynthesis: prototypic metabolic malformation syndromes *Human Molecular Genetics,* 2003 **12**: R75-R88

[12] Porter, Forbes D. Malformation syndromes due to inborn errors of cholesterol synthesis. *J. Clin. Invest.* 2002 **110**:715-724

[13]Tierney, E, *et al.* Behavior phenotype in the RHS/Smith -Lemli -Opitz Syndrome. *Am. J. Med. Genet.* 2001 **98**: 191-200

[14] Riccomagno, Martin M, Martinu, Lenka, *et al.* Specification of the mammalian cochlea is dependent on Sonic hedgehog *Genes and Develop.*2002 16,18: 2365-2378,

[15] Ramalho-Santos, Miguel, Melton, Douglas, and McMahon, Andrew P. Hedgehog signals regulate multiple aspects of gastrointestinal development. *Published WWW May 2000*

[16]Oro AE, Higgins K. 2003. Hair cycle regulation of Hedgehog Signal Reception. *Dev. Biol.* 2000 Mar; **255(2)**:238-48

[17]Allen M, et al. Hedgehog Signaling Regulates Sebaceous Gland Development. *Am J Pathol.*2003 Dec;**163(6)**:2173-8

[18]Kelley, Richard I, Hennekam Raoul C M. The Smith-Lemli-Opitz syndrome *J Med Genet* 2000;**37**:321-335 (May)

Pet Action Shots/Phyllis Ensley

Shiny coat, clear eyes, pink tongue . . .
this Havanese is the picture of good health

Chapter 7

Preventative Medicine...
Keeping Your Havanese Healthy
– Joanne V. Baldwin DVM

If you've purchased a puppy from sound, health-tested lines, *keeping* him healthy is up to you. Good nutrition, adequate exercise and attention, protection from infectious disease, both internal and external parasite control, and an annual checkup by a competent veterinarian are the best preventative medicine.

If you have purchased your Havanese from an ethical breeder, he will have had his first, and possibly second, set of "puppy shots" when you bring him home and you should get a dated record of the vaccinations given. He should also have been wormed at least twice, been given a "well-puppy checkup" by the breeder's vet, and those records should be included along with his AKC paperwork, so you can bring them along on his first vet visit.

Finding a Veterinarian

The time to find a vet is *before* you get the puppy home, not after. If you do not already have a pet at home and a vet you are comfortable with, you'll want to "shop around" before choosing one.

You can start by asking friends in your area which vets they use, or you can contact your local kennel club for suggestions. (Show breeders spend a lot of money on veterinary care compared to the rest of the world, and invariably hold strong opinions about who's good and who's not.) You can visit the vet's office in person and talk to the staff, or you can call. Some vets allow the owner in the examination room with their pet, and some do not. Decide which you prefer and ask about their policy in this regard beforehand. (Some vets are loathe to allow the owner in the exam room for liability reasons so, if you are allowed in, it is best to keep a low profile and not get in the way.)

You will also want to explain, before scheduling an appointment, that many Havanese owners have reported reactions to both 7-in-one vaccines and to some anesthetic protocols. If the vet pooh-poohs this, the safest course of action is to take your business elsewhere. Closed-mindedness is not a character trait you want in your dog's primary care physician!

Ask if the vet has reviewed the most recent canine vaccination protocols from the AAHA (American Animal Hospital Association.)[2] (The answer to this question should *not* be "Huh?") Our knowledge base on duration of immunity is rapidly expanding and your veterinarian should be familiar with current research.

And last, but not least, choose a vet whose personal style you are comfortable with - some clinics are quite formal in approach, whereas others are decidedly casual, and often have furry "clinic mascots" who more or less have the run of the place, which some people like and others do not. As

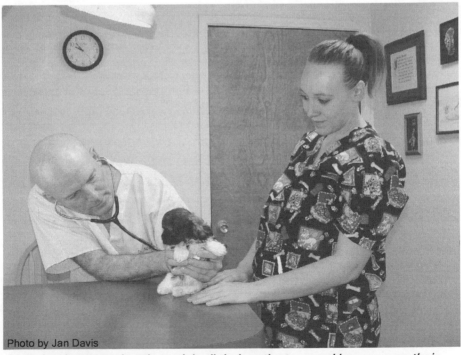

Photo by Jan Davis

Veterinarians say that they wish all their patients were Havanese as their sweet natures make them a pleasure to treat.

Core Havanese Puppy Vaccination Protocol

- *7-8 wks:*   Distemper/Parvo Vaccine
- *10-11 wks:* Distemper/Parvo/Parainfluenza/Adeno2. (Either as a 5 – way injection, or as a distemper/parvo injection and an intranasal which includes Adeno2, parainfluenza and Bordetella)
- *13-14 wk:* Repeat 10-11 wk vaccination
- *16-17 wks:* Rabies

- *1 year later:* Distemper/Adeno2/Parainfluenza /Parvovirus.
  Wait 3 weeks then Booster Rabies 3 year vaccination (if permitted by law...some states require annual Rabies vaccination.)

this will hopefully be a long-term relationship, it's best to find a vet whose personal style, and that of his staff, best fits your own.

Vaccinating Your Havanese

There have been numerous reports of vaccination reactions, some quite severe, in Havanese. Although the evidence is anecdotal, it is prudent to consider the Havanese to be a vaccine-sensitive breed, and to vaccinate accordingly. Most of the Havanese puppies who've had vaccination reactions were given 7-in-one vaccines, and the Leptospirosis component is often suspected to be the offending antigen. Lepto is caused by a bacteria *not* a virus, is treatable with antibiotics, and many breeds of dogs may be sensitive to the vaccine. (Ask your vet when he last treated a case of Lepto *in a dog*. If he can't remember, or if Lyndon Johnson was occupying the White House at the time, the risk to the puppy from a vaccine reaction probably outweighs his risk of contracting Lepto.)

The use of Lepto bacterin is not recommended for Havanese unless faced with an outbreak; even then it should be given separately from all other vaccines at least 3 weeks apart from any other vaccination and *never* before 9 weeks of age. If Lepto is given, the vet should make certain that the bacterin used actually contains the serovar(s) causing the outbreak, or it will be ineffective.

Always wait at least three weeks between vaccinations, to allow the immune system to recover before the next onslaught, and *never* allow the puppy to be given its first rabies shot at the same time as the third "puppy shot." The possibility of overloading the immune system here is simply not worth the inconvenience of a another trip. Note that some states still require annual Rabies vaccination, by law, even though there are vaccines available that have proven 3 year duration of immunity, by challenge.

Some vets will still vaccinate for Corona virus, although the routine use of this vaccine is currently considered, at best, unnecessary.[1] You have the right to refuse Corona vaccination and should insist that it be excluded from any vaccination. Non-core vaccines may be recommended and can be considered, based on risk assessment for your dog in your local area. An example would be Lyme vaccine for dogs in Northeast where Lyme is endemic and dogs exposed to ticks are at risk.

Until fairly recently, it was recommended that dogs receive a full series of vaccinations annually. The results of a long-term study published by the AAHA (and widely available to all vets nationwide) indicates that this is probably overkill, as most dogs maintain an adequate titer for several years after vaccination.[2] This is something you may want to discuss with your vet. Generally speaking, vets and breeders who have been around long enough to remember when puppies died gruesome and painful deaths from diseases like distemper and parvo, in spite of all the heroic efforts to save them, are most likely to err on the side of over-vaccination, while younger vets and breeders are less likely to do so. If you and your vet decide *not* to vaccinate annually, it may be advisable to run an annual titer to assess likely protection. As of this writing, there are available distemper, adeno2, parainfluenza, parvo vaccines that have a 3 year duration of immunity, by challenge, and are so labeled. In any case, **an annual veterinary checkup is essential for your Havanese if you wish to keep him healthy**.

Anesthesia

A healthy Havanese will rarely require anesthesia for any reason other than spaying or neutering, or for dental work, but this is a place where you do need to be careful. An alarming number of Havanese owners have re-ported problems encountered by their dogs while under anesthesia, and your vet should be aware of this before he puts yours under for any reason. Some of these problems can be avoided by taking certain precautions be-forehand.

First, **request a blood panel before EVER considering anesthesia for a Havanese**, as this is a breed in which liver and heart problems are not un-common. At minimum, this should include a CBC and pre-anesthetic chem-istry panel. A complete physical should be done as well at the same time.

A safe method of anesthetizing a Havanese, is masking the dog down with isoflurane (alternatively, sevoflurane may be used) and then to intubate when the dog is anesthetized. It admittedly takes a little longer to mask a dog down than to induce anesthesia with injectable chemicals, but this is offset by the control that gas anesthesia provides. Pain medication, such as Butorphanol, given 15 or 20 minutes before anesthetizing a dog will often smooth the induction period. (In most cases, pain control should be part of surgical procedures as dogs recover much better if they are not in pain. If your vet does not suggest It, ask if post-operative pain medications are ap-propriate.) In the case of a particularly uncooperative dog (rare in a Hava-nese) Propofol, an intravenous anesthetic, can be used for induction, as its duration is less than 5 minutes, so if there is any reaction the dog can be maintained for the few minutes required for the drug to be cleared from the system.

Parasite Control

Not so long ago parasites, both internal and external, were a major problem for dogs and owners alike, especially in the South, where fleas drove dogs to distraction year round and hookworm and whipworm infesta-tions were virtually impossible to control. Toxic sprays, powders, dips, shampoos, nasty potions, and even flea bombs (with which you poisoned your entire house) represented the arsenal with which man sought to win the age-old battle against parasites on and in the domestic dog.

Today's Havanese owner is far luckier in that regard. Internal parasites can be easily controlled by the use of once-a-month tablets, such as Interceptor and Heartgard, that prevent infestation by deadly heartworms, as well as roundworms, hookworms and, with Interceptor, whipworms. An annual heartworm check is recommended even with year round use of heartworm preventative. Newer in-house tests combine the test for heartworm with tests for Lyme disease and Ehrichia (both tick borne diseases) and give results in less than ten minutes.

Likewise, external parasites like fleas and ticks can be kept in check by the application of a topical insecticide, such as Frontline (effective against fleas and ticks) or Advantage (fleas only), applied once a month on the skin between the dog's shoulder blades. These topicals are far safer both for dogs and humans than anything used previously, can be used year-round if needed, and Havanese seem to tolerate them well. Be wary of some of the "look alike" products available over-the-counter which contain potentially toxic chemicals (such as permethrin, which can be lethal to cats, for example) and are appear to be less effective than Frontline or Advantage.

The only parasite that seems to have escaped the new broad-spectrum monthly treatments is the tapeworm. Should you notice what look like small flat grains of rice in the stool of your Havanese, or clinging to the fur on his backside, consult your veterinarian, who will prescribe the appropriate treatment. Do not attempt to eradicate tapeworms yourself - nothing you can buy over-the-counter is particularly effective. Tapeworms are most commonly transmitted by infected fleas. It should also be mentioned that care must be taken when ordering drugs from some online pharmacies which have been caught offering counterfeit, or imported and unapproved products.

Poisoning

Accidental poisoning is far easier to prevent than to treat, but should you suspect your dog has ingested or been exposed to a poisonous substance, *immediately* call the nearest poison-control hotline or 24 hour emergency vet clinic and tell them exactly what the dog has come in contact with.

Appropriate emergency treatment depends entirely on the toxin, and this is a case where doing the *wrong* thing can be worse than doing nothing at all.

Using a Thermometer

If you suspect your Havanese is not feeling well, it is a good idea to take his temperature *before* calling the vet, as he will be in a better position to advise you with this information factored in. (There is a big difference, for example, between a puppy who has just vomited with a normal temperature versus one who has just vomited and has a temperature of 104.5!!)

Normal temperature for a dog is around 101.5, taken rectally with a digital thermometer you can buy at the drugstore. Lubricating it first with a little Vaseline helps.

It's probably wise to take your dog's temperature a time or two when he is feeling fine and record it, so you know what is normal for him, as individuals dogs may vary somewhat.

Emergencies

Every responsible Havanese owner needs to have, prominently posted in an easily-seen location near the phone, several phone numbers, along with the addresses for each. The first is, of course, your own vet, who probably won't be available in the middle of the night.

So the *second* number you need is that of the nearest 24 hour emergency vet clinic. These clinics, which are a fairly new phenomenon, are a Godsend. Ask your vet to recommend the nearest one, *and find out well in advance of needing their services exactly how to get there*. If it is a true emergency, you will be panicked enough already, and thumbing through the yellow pages and then getting lost on your way to a clinic you've never been

---

Emergency Phone Numbers (Post near phone!!):

Puppy's regular vet:

24-hour emergency clinic:

Poison control hotline:

Puppy's breeder:

---

to with a perilously ill dog in the car could end up costing your Havanese his life.

The third number you need to have posted is that of the poison-control center hotline mentioned above. Make sure the center whose number you post has staff available day and night. When you really need help, the *last* thing you need is a recorded message. (If you do need to call a poison-control hotline, have your credit card handy, as most charge a nominal fee for the call.)

The last number you need to have posted is that of your breeder. Some "emergencies" are not veterinary in nature, but perhaps behavioral or downright silly, and these are where an experienced and caring breeder is often more help than anyone else.

References

1. http://www.ivis.org/advances/Infect_Dis_Carmichael/schultz/chapter_frm.asp?LA=1
2. http://www.vin.com/proceedings/Proceedings.plx?CID=WSAVA2002&PID=2614

Photo by Ashby

Havanese color often changes as the dogs mature. These two pictures are of the same bitch.

Top picture of her as a young show dog and, to left, as a mature brood bitch.

Photo by Peggy Baird

122

Chapter 8

The Well-Groomed Havanese

One of the greatest misconceptions about the Havanese is that it is an "easy care" or a "no-groom" breed. Over an average lifespan, a well-cared-for Havanese will require about 750 baths and will need brushing anywhere from 1,500 (that's about twice a week) to 5,400 times (brushing daily) to keep him clean and mat-free...if you really don't enjoy grooming, this is simply not the right breed for you, and you might as well know that right out of the gate.

With the right equipment, and a fair amount of self-discipline, however, any Havanese owner can keep their pet looking like a show dog without relying on the services of a professional groomer. Unlike the elaborate sculpting, clipping, and/or stripping required in some breeds to make pets even vaguely resemble their counterparts seen at dog shows, weekly bathing, with a good shampoo and conditioner, and diligent - and frequent - brushing are all that is required of the Havanese, assuming the coat is correct to begin with. Scissor the feet into a neat round shape, and he's in "show trim"!

On the other hand, Havanese with excessively curly or frizzy coats, or those with a cottony texture that mats before your very eyes, will be far beyond the capabilities of the average owner to maintain at full length no matter *how* diligent one is. These dogs are probably better maintained in a short "puppy-cut" by a professional groomer, although they will require bathing and frequent brushing between visits, as these coats will mat even if they are only an inch or two long.

If this "short, fluffy look" is not what you had envisioned for your Havanese, it is wise to look carefully at the coats of *both* parents before purchasing a pup, as coat texture, density, and the amount of wave carried in the coat are all genetically determined. (If you are already saddled with a high-maintenance coat on your Havanese and don't *want* to keep it very short, it should be noted that these coats will also cord, provided they are soft and, once corded, you can let it grow as long as you'd like without brushing. A coarse, frizzy, and/or brittle coat will not cord satisfactorily - but then again, it won't mat, either.)

The Puppy Trim

If you have decided that, for whatever reason, you are going to employ the services of a professional groomer and keep your Havanese in a puppy trim, you will have to decide beforehand exactly what that means to you and how you visualize it. Dog groomers want to please their clients and, operating within the constraints of coat texture and length, they will usually try to give the client what they want. But in all fairness, *dog groomers are not mind-readers*; they need to know precisely what the client wants *before* they start to remove hair. So bring a photograph or two along illustrating how you wish your dog to look. (If the groomer is insulted, find another groomer. Closed-mindedness is no more desirable a trait in a groomer than it is in a vet.)

Failure to take this precaution can have disastrous consequences. Bear in mind that many groomers have never *seen* a Havanese, much less groomed one. Those who are familiar with the breed may have other clients whose idea of a Havanese puppy trim is nothing like yours. If the groomer shaves your dog's face and feet like Poodle and ties bows in his ears, or cuts bangs that strongly resemble those made famous by the late Mamie Eisenhower, you will have to live with the results for many weeks until it grows out, and you will have no one but yourself to blame.

The traditional Havanese puppy trim takes the body coat down with a 7F or 4F blade (the 4F will be slightly longer) and clips or scissors the legs into straight columns ending in rounded, *scissored,* not closely clipped, feet. The tail is generally left natural, with the plume shortened a bit if necessary to balance the rest of the dog. Pompoms are a dumb idea on a Havanese.

The feathering on the ears is left natural like the tail but shortened a bit if needed. The muzzle furnishings should be scissored into a neatly rounded shape. The inside corners of the eyes may be trimmed, and the head furnishings can be shortened, and thinned with a thinning shears if they are so heavy as to obscure vision.

Allowing the head furnishings to taper longer toward the outside, blending into the furnishings of the ears, while shortening the center, will preserve the typical Havanese expression, while allowing for unobstructed vision. Scissoring the head furnishings into a tight round topknot like a pet Poodle, on the other hand, will completely eradicate breed type, and if it doesn't *look* like a Havanese, why have one?

This 2 year old Havanese, looks like an adorable puppy in this cut.

One caveat, however: If your dog has a truly ideal coat in good condition - soft, silky and wavy without a tremendous amount of crimp - the overall effect of a puppy trim using a clippers will remind you forcibly of the old seventies "shag" hairdo - it won't fluff out as you'd hoped, but rather it will just lie there, flat as a pancake, in a zillion different lengths, and it's not particularly cute. It is the "crimp", which are the s-curves along each hair strand, that causes the coat to stand out from the body - the less crimp (in other words, the larger each S) the flatter the hair will lie. (That's why frizzy hair, which contains many little s-curves per strand, tends to puff out in spite of one's best efforts to make it lie down, no matter how soft the hair.)

These ideal coats look far better if the body coat is *not* trimmed with a clipper, but rather is scissored to four or five inches all over so that it still falls easily into a part down the center of the back, with the neck, underline, legs, ears, and head furnishings trimmed neatly to about the same length. The lucky owner of a Havanese with this coat can usually manage to achieve this look themselves at home with minimal skill, a greyhound comb, and a sharp scissors. Here's the technique:

You simply hold sections of hair straight out with the comb, and trim it to the same length all over. The underside and leg furnishings can be trimmed into a neat line.

The feet and muzzle are scissored into a full rounded shape, and the tail can be left alone to fall over the back, neatened slightly. The head furnishings can be trimmed as in the Puppy Clip. The hair under the tail can be trimmed as short as needed for good hygiene. Freshly bathed and blown dry, the overall effect will be that of a six-month old puppy ready for his first dog show, and it is charming.

Brushing 101

If trained early, your Havanese will come to enjoy a daily 10 or 15-minute grooming session, and so will you. This is all it takes to keep his coat in perfect condition and tangle-free, no matter what its length. It will also allow you, the owner, to notice anything physical that may be amiss before it gets out of hand, because you will go over every inch of him every day. This is called "line-brushing", and it is the technique used by professional handlers to maintain the glorious flowing coats on show dogs.

126

You might as well start as soon as you get him, although you will be hard-pressed to make the session last 10 minutes until his coat grows a little. (This is just as well, as puppies have short attention spans, and 3-5 minutes is probably as long as he can be realistically persuaded to hold still!)

The first thing you need is a suitable table, as this will make the job much easier for both of you. A small folding "ringside grooming table" can be purchased through many dog supply catalogues, or a sturdy wooden TV tray will work also. *Sturdy* is the critical word here, because no dog will feel secure enough to lie still on a wobbly table.

You will also need a *soft* pin brush (not really necessary for a very young puppy but get one anyway), a greyhound comb (this is simply a metal comb with fine teeth on one half and coarser ones on the other), and a spray bottle of water, to which you may add a little conditioner or tangle-remover. You may also choose to use a commercially prepared leave-in conditioner/detangler.

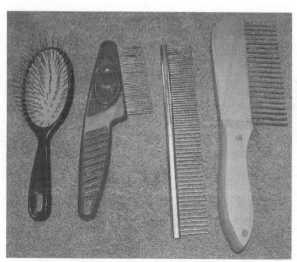

A soft pin brush, fine comb, greyhound comb and coarse comb

Place your table in front of a comfortable chair (facing the TV works just fine) and cover it with a towel. Sit down and place the puppy on the table.

 Teach the puppy to lie on his side quietly, holding the palm of one hand flat across his shoulder and ribcage and stroking him gently with the other until he relaxes. (You may have to work on this step a few times before beginning to brush, but the puppy will soon get the hang of it, and come to enjoy it.)

Lightly mist the rear leg with the spray bottle (never, ever, brush a dry Havanese as it will break coat) and starting with the foot, comb carefully and lightly through the coat in horizontal "lines" no wider than an inch, always combing downward and working from left to right, layer after layer, gently untangling as needed, working your way up the leg toward the hip. Lift the leg gently and comb through the inside of the opposite rear leg. Once the rear leg is done, mist the tail, comb through that, and then move on to the body.

Working from the tummy upward toward the spine, still working in narrow lines (no wider than an inch) move gently from left to right along the length of the body, misting lightly as you go. On an older dog, you may use the pin brush to line-brush the body, using the comb only when needed to gently tease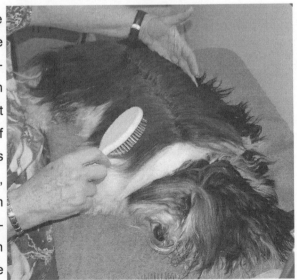

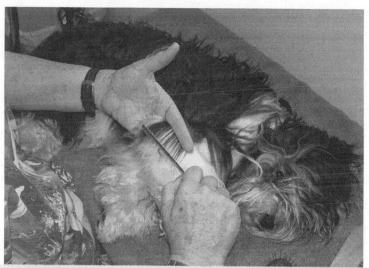

Grip coat between comb and skin to make tangle removal painless.

apart any small tangles, and to comb through a section when finished to make sure you haven't missed any tangles. (If you run into one, do *not* pull outward with the comb, as you will pull out hair from the roots, and your Havanese will protest loudly. Instead, stop, mist the area again, tease it apart gently with your fingers if you need to, then comb through it, laying it down onto the already-brushed portion.)

Mist the front leg lightly, and proceed as you did with the rear leg, mak-

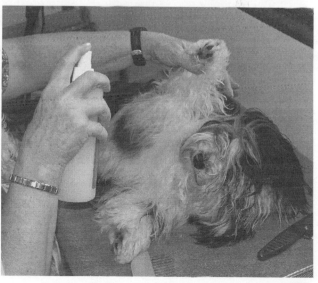

ing sure to comb through the area under the elbow and between the front legs.

Mist the chest and neck next, and line-brush as you did with the body, starting with the lower chest and working up the neck.

Lightly mist the

puppy's head and use the comb to carefully comb through the area under the ear; this is a good time to check and see if the ears need attention. Comb the side of the head next, still working in narrow lines from the bottom up, making sure catch any tangles that may be under the chin.

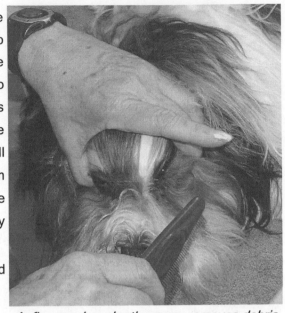

Now turn him over and repeat the entire process.

A fine comb under the eyes removes debris

Stand him up on the table, brush through him one last time, and praise him lavishly. This is a good time to reward him with a favorite treat.

If you make it a habit to do this *every day,* you will never have to fight with the dog, as there will be never be any mats to brush out, and the experience will be both positive and relaxing for you and your Havanese.

If you honestly can't manage it daily, try for a at least a couple times a week, which will usually be OK, unless your Havanese is changing from puppy coat to adult coat, during which time you really do need to go through him once a day or you will have a disaster on your hands that may require professional assistance.

A Word on Brushes

You will find an amazing array of brushes available for dogs, and deciding which one to choose can be daunting.

Most professional handlers swear by the soft pin brush, and use it almost exclusively on long coated dogs. Make sure the one you buy is soft, however - the "pins" are imbedded in a rubber base, and some are painfully stiff. An acceptable alternative may be the porcupine brush, which contains long pin bristles surrounded by softer, shorter bristles. The ubiquitous slicker brush is totally *useless* on a Havanese coat - it will brush the top of the coat, but its short, bent wire bristles never get all the way through, where mats actually form, and it will break hair. (It is, however, very useful for removing dog hair from carpeting!)

Bathing, Nail Trimming , Etc...

Aside from brushing, there is a fair amount of grooming that is needed to keep your Havanese in good condition. In order to keep your dog looking and smelling his best he will need to be bathed weekly, after brushing, with a good shampoo and conditioner. There is no single product or brand of product that works best on all Havanese, so you will have to experiment a little until you come up with what works best for your dog and his particular coat texture, and follow the directions on the label. Baby shampoos work well for young puppies, as they are mild and do not sting the eyes. Most Havanese will easily fit in a laundry sink, and that is the best place to bathe them. A drop of mineral oil in each eye will protect the eyes from shampoo, and a cotton ball in each ear will keep the inner ear dry, which will help avoid ear infection.

After shampooing, rinse thoroughly and then, when you think the dog is totally rinsed, rinse again. Failure to rinse completely is probably the commonest cause of an "itchy" dog, and one that is easily avoided.

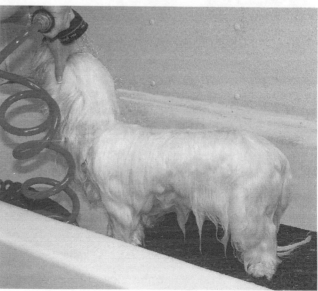

Once bathed, unless you live in a very hot and dry climate, you will want to blow-dry your Havanese. Squeezing out the excess water and then wrapping him in a large towel like a burrito for a few minutes after bathing will cut drying time. Use a dryer made specifically for dogs, as they use more air flow and less heat than those made for people. A small tabletop dog dryer on a stand can be purchased inexpensively, and will be adequate for a single dog. Teach your Havanese to lie quietly on a towel-covered table while wrapped in a second dry towel for drying the same as you would for line brushing, starting with the head and unwrapping as you dry. Use a pin brush to go through the coat while you are drying , using more or less the same procedure, but working from front to back this time. With young puppies, a boar bristle brush works well and is easier on tender puppy skin.

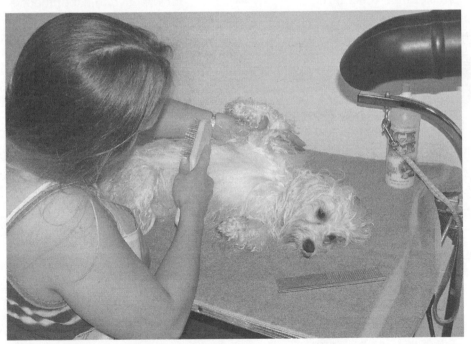

In addition to a weekly bath, a Havanese needs the excess hair pulled from the ear canal to help avoid ear infections. This is honestly painless for the dog, although it is hard to believe. Your vet can show you how to do it. Check the ear for any signs of inflammation or excessive wax. A healthy ear should have no odor, and the skin should be pink with little or no visible wax. Ear infections are usually easier (and cheaper!) to avoid than to treat.

Your Havanese will need to have his nails trimmed every other week or so, and bath time is the logical time to do it. A nail trimmer with a guard that does not allow you to accidentally remove too much is a good idea for the novice. If you do cut too close, and the nail bleeds, you can easily staunch the blood flow with a little styptic powder, which you should always have handy. Many Havanese breeders leave the dewclaws (these are really vestigial "thumbs" on a dog) on their puppies, as there is no really good reason to remove them, but you do need to trim that nail as well.

The hair on the inside corner of the eye may be trimmed, or it may be allowed to grow long and blend Into the muzzle furnishings. Be apprised that once trimmed, you must continue to keep it trimmed, so decide which you prefer and stick with it. A flea comb works better than anything for cleaning the dried matter that collects on the inside corners of the eyes. You will also want to do some trimming around the anal and genital areas to keep your Havanese

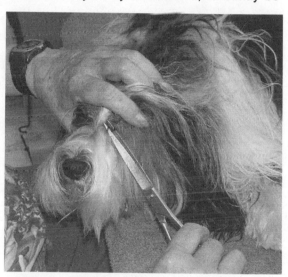

Covering the eye to keep it closed both protects the eye and prevents the "menace reflex" triggered by objects close to the eyes.

clean, and this can be easily accomplished with a scissors or thinning shears and a steady hand.

Havanese feet need to be trimmed as well. Untrimmed, the hair on the bottoms of the feet will grow to cover the pads, and the dog will track in both mud and water. A small scissors will do the job, or you can purchase a little battery-operated clipper that fits in the palm of your hand to remove the hair between the pads. (It is impossible to accidentally cut the pad with one of these, so it's a good idea for that reason. Dogs quickly get used to the little buzzing noise it makes.)

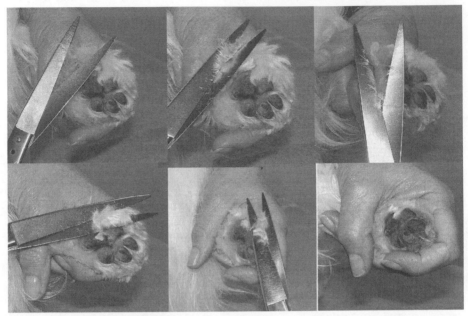

Photo montage by Stephanie Foard

The hair around the feet should also be trimmed for housekeeping purposes as well. The easiest way to do this is to slide your hand straight down the leg until only the pads are exposed in the circle made by your thumb and forefinger. Trim off all the hair that extends beyond this circle, and the result will be a nice tidy round foot. The best time to do this is right after blow-drying, when the feet are clean and dry.

This small, battery operated clipper is great for trimming the bottoms of the paws and in between the pads. Most dogs quickly learn to tolerate it's buzzing noise.

Grooming Equipment List

Grooming table
Shampoo
Conditioner
Detangler/conditioner spray
Greyhound comb
Soft pin-brush
Nylon pin/boar bristle combination brush

Cotton balls
Mineral oil
Chamois-type drying sponge
Soft bath-size towels
Dog dryer on stand
Flea comb
Nail trimmer
Styptic powder

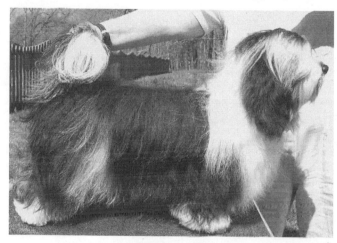

Grooming sessions over and ready for Glamour Shots

This young Havanese has cute, bouncy, baby cords.

Photo by Terri Pike

Photo by Diane Klumb

Mature corded Havanese with floor length cords.

Chapter 9

The Corded Havanese

The AKC Standard for the Havanese allows for both a corded and a brushed coat and, although many owners are unaware of it, cording has been an accepted option in the Havanese breed in the United States since the very first HCA Standard was written in 1981. As with his cousin the Poodle, the historical basis for cording the Havanese is found in references dating back to the 1800s, when corded dogs were a bit of a fad in Europe.

Some owners will argue that a corded coat is unnatural in a breed purported to be a "natural dog" but, every owner can attest, any Havanese of proper coat texture will cord if allowed to do so - in fact, much of the grooming that this breed requires reflects no more than an ongoing effort to *prevent* the Havanese coat from cording! Cords are no more nor less than organized mats, and separating these mats into tidy tendrils is surely no less natural than brushing them out completely, as the tendency for the mats to form in the first place is an entirely natural process.

Whether one wishes to keep one's Havanese in brushed coat or corded is largely a matter of personal preference, as both are considered equally correct for the breed in the show ring - in fact, several of the top winning Havanese in the first few years following the breed's acceptance into the AKC Toy Group have been corded.

Additionally, pet owners who simply do not wish to put in the considerable amount of time required to maintain the brushed coat at its natural length, but feel the short fluffy pet trim detracts from the "shaggy dog" look that attracted to them to the breed in the first place, find cording to be a good solution to their brushing woes.

Cording Basics

A fair number of pet owners have seen corded Havanese at shows, either in person or on TV and, after watching them trotting around the ring, cords swinging, decide they'd like to try it on their own dog, but have no idea where to start. Most assume that cording is difficult to effect and maintain, and way beyond their capabilities.

Cording a Havanese is actually fun, and not difficult at all. It is well within the capabilities of the average pet owner. Once corded, there is little work required to maintain this traffic-stopping look, outside of a bath. It *does,* however, require a fair amount of patience on the owner's part, especially in the first few months, when they are going through the "lumpy mattress stage", which is not particularly attractive, even to hard-core fans of the corded Havanese.

The advantages that corded Havanese maintain over their larger corded compatriots - the Puli, the Komondor, and the Poodle - is that because of both their size and coat texture, it takes a lot less time to completely cord a Havanese and, once corded, it takes a lot less time to bathe and dry them. (Drying an entire Havanese is like drying one leg on a Komondor!)

When it comes to cording, misconceptions abound. A corded Havanese will invariably draw the following questions:

"Do you have to brush those out every time you give him a bath?" *(No, you bathe him cords and all, once a week - it's just like hand-washing a sweater.)*

"Do you have to twist each one into a string like that?" *(No, they form all by themselves, you just separate them.)*

"How many days does it take to *dry* that dog?" *(A couple hours if you use a fan and a blow-dryer.)*

"Bet that takes a lot of time, huh?" *(No more time than brushing. Quite a bit less time once they are established.)*

"Don't you get a lot of skin problems with cords?" (*No, actually the skin is easy to see and gets good airflow. Corded dogs rarely suffer from skin problems.*)

"Whoa, are those *dreads*, man?" *(Yup. Cords are indeed little doggy dreadlocks.)*

One of the most common misconceptions about cords on a Havanese is that they are strands of twisted hair. They are not. The hair does *not* twist around itself to form cords in this breed, although it may in others. A parti-colored Havanese, when corded, will have some cords that are neatly and clearly striped. If the hair was actually twisting, these black-and-white cords would look like candy-canes, but they do not - instead, the stripes are vertical, and run the length of the cord. So what is *really* happening when a cord forms?

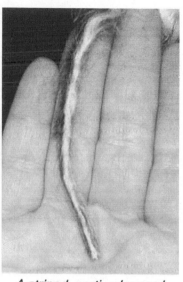

A striped, parti-color cord

In order to understand cords, you first need to understand what makes up a strand of hair. Each hair consists of several layers:

•The *medulla*, the very center of the hair shaft, is a cellularly active canal made up of collagenous protein; the ability of light to pass through this canal determines the color of the hair.

•Surrounding the medulla is the *cortex*. This layer is composed of millions of protein chains. The amount of water in the hair shaft is relative to the amount of protein in the cortical layers. Healthy hair contains approximately 10% to 20% of its weight in water.

• The *cuticle* is the outermost layer of the hair shaft. This is a hard transparent shingle-like layer much like the shingles on the roof of a house, or the scales on a fish. The cuticle layer, because of its flattened overlapping structure, makes the hair shaft hydrophobic (water resistant). The function of the cuticle is to protect the layers beneath it.

Variations in the structure of the cuticle are responsible for most of the differences in hair texture, while variations in the medulla are responsible for what we perceive as hair color. In humans, these differences are primarily ethnic; in dogs, they vary from breed to breed. It is the structure of the Havanese cuticle that allows a cord to form. The straighter the hair, the flatter the cuticle scales lie on the hair shaft. Wherever the hair has a wave in it, the scales on the shaft are forced open at that point. (This is why stick-straight hair is inevitably shinier than wavy hair, incidentally - the flatter the scales, the better they reflect light.)

In addition, the sebaceous glands produce oil which lubricates the hair, sealing the cuticle. As the wavy Havanese coat does not have a lot of weight to hold it down, nor a lot of natural oil (which is why Havanese have little doggy odor), conditioning products and constant brushing of the hair are needed to keep the scales lying flat.

When each hair is not continually brushed in the same direction as the ones next to it, they become disorganized, and the lack of weight causes some hairs to scrunch up like ribbon candy. The opened scales on these strands then "catch" onto the ones next to them, precisely like Velcro, forming mats. The reason these mats can be pulled apart into cords is because the hairs are for the most part attached to each other vertically, along their length. (This is why a parti-colored cord is striped lengthwise rather than in a spiral.) The scrunching is why a cord is initially shorter than the hair that goes into it - these are the "loops" in the "hook and loop" Velcro process. The open scales of the wavy hairs that don't scrunch form the "hooks", and account for the wisps of hair that extend beyond the corded part. As each individual hair is shed, it stays in the cord, and is replaced by another new hair, which then works its way into the existing cord when it gets long enough. For this reason, cords will continue to grow longer throughout the life of the dog, at a rate of approximately 4-6 inches per year.

Dogs with denser hair (containing more hair follicles per square inch -

what is referred to as a "good double coat" in this breed) will form mats faster than dogs with less hair for obvious reasons, and will cord in a heartbeat. It is a commonly held belief that curlier coats will cord readily, while the "ideal" wavy coats will not, but this has simply not proven to be the case in Havanese. Likewise the myth that curly coats are necessary in order to preserve coat density has proven to be untrue in this breed. Coat density and the amount of curl in a coat have long been known by canine geneticists to be controlled by different genes, and these genes are inherited independently. (In fact, some of the *densest* coats in the world of dogs, Chow Chows and Keeshonden, are entirely without curl.) A dense, silky Havanese coat with no discernable curl will cord beautifully, while a thin but curly coat will produce less than spectacular results. A coarse, wiry coat will not cord at all, as the texture is wrong. A flat, single Havanese coat *will* cord, but the cords will be few and far between! (As these coats are remarkably easy to maintain brushed and full length, and will look prettier brushed than corded, there is little reason to cord them anyway.)

There are two proven methods for cording a Havanese, and both will produce identical results in the end. Which you choose is largely a matter of temperament - yours, not the dog's.

Method One: Traditional Cording

Traditional cording, which is the method used on most of the corded breeds, consists of allowing mats to form by bathing the dog without brushing him first, and then drying the dog thoroughly without brushing. This process is repeated weekly, and the dog is misted with plain water daily between baths. The first mats will start to form (often on the back end) within the first week or two, depending on the coat texture. These "wads" are then misted and pulled apart with the fingers into smaller wads, about the size of a nickel at the base, as they form. One would expect this to be painful for the dog, but it is not. If a mat won't split easily, and the dog protests when you try, you can easily slice through it *from the skin outward*, using one side of an open scissors in a sawing motion. This happens most often near the ears, where the mats often form with horizontal as well as vertical attachments.

Frequent bathing and misting several times a day will speed the process considerably. Each bath will cause these puffy wads to tighten and become denser and thinner until they start turning into actual cords, which is why you don't want to make them too thin to begin with. The uncorded, loose hair between the mats will eventually work its way into the cords already formed. It is important to know that the cord does not form right to the skin - there is always about a half-inch of uncorded hair before the beginning of the cord, no matter what its length or how tight the rest of the cord is. Some Havanese, depending on their individual coat types, will form cords almost on their own, without much splitting except around the legs, while others will need constant work to break up the lumps of hair as they form.

Using the traditional cording process, it will probably take close to a year before a Havanese is attractively corded, with cords about 4-6 inches long. Prior to that, he will appear "lumpy" and matted, with some corded and some uncorded hair. (Most of the earliest cords will be toward the back end of a Havanese, and most of the uncorded hair will be on the shoulders, with the area of silky hair on top of the shoulders and often the head being invariably the last to cord.) Your family, friends, and neighbors will very likely be unsupportive, insisting that "those are *mats*, not cords!" and you might as well be prepared for this right out the gate. It takes both patience and sheer *sisu* to cord a Havanese in the teeth of this sort of criticism and, combined with the prospect of many months of living with a really unattractive dog, many owners simply give up. For this reason, you may want to consider Method Two.

Method Two: Speed-cording

Author's note: Speed-cording was first explained to me by a charming Puli owner back when I was cording my first Havanese; I listened carefully, examined his beautifully speed-corded dog, and corded four dogs by the

142

traditional method before gathering the courage to attempt it. In each case it took almost a year to go from fully brushed to fully corded. I finally decided to give the speed-cording method a try.

Ten weeks from the day I stopped brushing, I entered my first speed-corded dog, completely covered from head to tail in short bouncing cords, in the Havanese National Specialty.

The *technique* of speed-cording is simple; the hard part is actually convincing yourself to *do* it. Essentially, what one does is allow the dog to turn into *a solidly matted mass* over a period of 8-10 weeks, bathing and *thoroughly* drying him weekly, and misting daily. (It is probably best to keep your dog pretty close to home during this time, as absolutely *no one* will believe you if you explain to them that you are speed-cording your Havanese. Trust me on this.)

In fact, the longer you can make yourself wait (within limits, of course - a year is probably overkill!), and the more completely felted you let the dog get, the better the results

September 2004

January 2005

Speed cording transformation

seem to be. There is no such thing during this period as too much bathing or too much misting; these will increase the matting and tighten the cording quicker. So the choices are really "benign neglect" or "active neglect"...the latter will speed the process considerably!

Then, when you have reached the point of solid felt everywhere and you are pretty sure you have made a terrible mistake and his skin will be a disaster under there (it won't if you dry him thoroughly), you simply cut a grid all over the dog, much like you'd cut up a pan of brownies. This is the technique long used in traditional cording to separate the felted areas - the only difference is you are doing the whole dog rather than just a few areas.

You'll need a table, a pair of sharp scissors, (or maybe two pair of sharp scissors; and don't bother with expensive ones, as they will dull quickly) and a spray bottle of water. With the dog lying comfortably upright (not on his side) on the towel-covered table, starting at the occiput and working toward the tail, you slice through the felted mass *from the skin outward* with one blade of an open scissors using a sawing motion, following a line along the vertebrae right to the base of the tail. This will divide the felt in half. Make your next line about an inch to the (dog's) right of the original one and parallel to it down the length of the dog. Follow that with another, again about an inch down and parallel to the one above it, continuing down the side of the dog. When one side is completed, do the other in the same manner. The body is now divided into horizontal layers. Then "cross-saw" outward at one inch intervals on each layer until the whole thing looks like a grid, or a pan of cut-up brownies, misting as you go. Occasionally you will have to use the scissors to actually *cut* through some areas, but saw with an open scissors wherever you can, following the direction of the hair as much as possible, as the cords will be longer that way. If you make a mistake, and cut off a scary-sized chunk by accident, don't panic- odds are it won't show!

Finish the body and then move onto the ears, legs, and tail, which are a little harder to do, but by this time you'll be pretty good at it. The whole project will take the better part of a weekend. Although it's not in the least bit painful for the dog, it is *boring* for him to lie on a table for hours on end and he'll get wiggly after a while, so you'll want to break it up into several sessions. It also helps to have an assistant on hand, for moral support if nothing else. (It is also easier to do the underside with a helper to hold the dog up on his hind legs while you cut a grid.)

When the grid is complete, and the felt is totally separated into pieces no smaller than an inch at the base all over, you round off the ends of these fluffy cords (there will be some seriously long hair sticking out of some of the ends if you started with a dog in full length coat) trim his feet and his private areas, and pop him into a tub of warm water, right up to his chin. Soak him for about ten minutes, then shampoo, rinse, condition, rinse again, blot out the excess water, blow dry and - voila! - you have a totally corded dog, honest to God. If the dog was completely matted, there will be little if any uncorded hair.

A Havanese who has been speed-corded will end up with exactly the same cords as one who was started traditionally - there will be a half inch of uncorded hair at the roots. As the hair grows out, and the cording process becomes automatic, the cords will get longer and longer. They will also tighten and become thinner, and any uncorded hair will eventually work its way into the existing cords, if you bathe and mist the dog frequently.

Bathing and Drying a Corded Havanese

Bathing a corded Havanese is a lot like washing a sweater by hand - fill a laundry tub with warm water (as warm as is comfortable for the dog) and soak him in it for a good ten minutes if you can, right up to his chin. A teaspoon of household chorine bleach per five gallons of water added to the laundry tub (the US Government recommended ratio for purifying drinking water) will go a long way to-

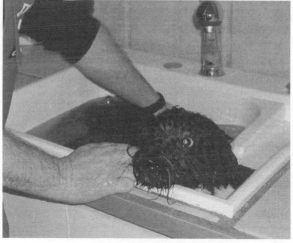

ward keeping a corded Havanese from smelling like mildew and will not harm the cords at all. (If you already have highly chlorinated city water, this may be unnecessary!)

Let the water out of the tub and apply shampoo to the cords, massaging it into the skin, paying special attention to the underside, especially on a male dog. Rinse thoroughly, add a good conditioner and leave it in for a few minutes. (Well-conditioned cords on a true black dog will look less "rusty" than dried-out ones, and well-conditioned white cords will attract less dirt. Conditioner will *not* cause the cords to unravel.) Rinse thoroughly. When the dog is completely rinsed out, rinse again.

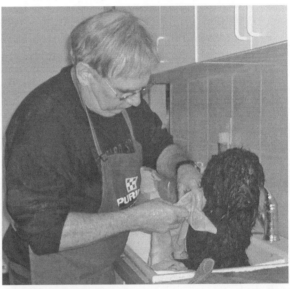

After rinsing, all excess water should be squeezed out of the cords *before* you take the dog out of the tub, or there will be floods of water everywhere. The easiest way to do this is to purchase a couple of those big super-thin colored sponges called "the Absorber" that come in a clear plastic tube in Wal-Mart's automotive section. (Designed for detailing cars, and no thicker than a chamois

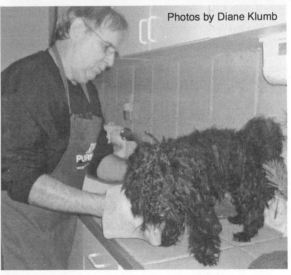

Photos by Diane Klumb

cloth, they will absorb their weight in water many times over and can be wrung out and used again and again. This will save you a dryer load of towels per bath, and the more time you spend wringing out the cords, the less time you'll spend drying.) When he is damp, but no longer dripping, take him out of the tub, wrap him in a thick towel and blot some more.

The dog can then be dried in a wire crate padded with a thick towel or two, using both a blow-dryer and a fan, while he takes a nap. Remember to check the air temperature frequently, as with all crate-drying, so as not to roast the dog and to replace the damp towel with dry ones as needed. Dryers like the Airforce, which do not have a heat setting, are safest. Once he is mostly dry (this will take a couple hours) he should be finished off by hand to make sure there are no damp spots left (usually the underside will still be damp) and this is a good time to do more cord-splitting. Any stray wisps protruding from the cords can be easily broken off with the fingers, causing no damage to the cord, and will give the dog a neater appearance. (If one is cording a pet, this can be done with a scissors, and the ends can be neatly rounded.)

A Few Extra Cording Notes:

Most Havanese owners prefer to keep the muzzle and chin area brushed out rather than corded for hygienic reasons, as dog food and cords don't mix well, and this is perfectly acceptable, even in the show ring.

Once the cords are well-formed, the pet owner can keep them at any length desired, as trimming the ends will *not* cause them to unravel. The corded dog destined for the show ring should be kept full length, and after a few years the cords will literally sweep the floor with spectacular effect.

Male dogs with long cords should have them tied up with scrunchies around the flanks when they go outside, to keep them clean. In wet weather the long skirting can be tied up as well, on both males and females. The soft brightly colored scrunchies made for little girls' ponytails work well.

Havanese cords are very strong, and will rarely break, even when tugged on by puppies. The occasional loss of a cord during play is nothing to be alarmed about, as it will probably not show anyway. If the cords start breaking off at the skin, however, it's because the dog is blowing coat, and the new hair is not growing in fast enough to keep up with the hair being shed. This happens often with bitches after heat or whelping, especially around the neck and shoulders, which can become quite bare, and there's not much you can do about it. New cords will eventually replace them. It is for this reason most corded Havanese are males or spayed bitches!

Should you decide you are tired of cords, you can always cut them off, and the coat will grow back to full length within the year. Once corded, though, a Havanese *cannot* be brushed back out.

Warning: cording a Havanese is addictive. Once you really get into it, you won't be able to stop until your dog is "perfect".

Black and white cords, soft and silky , dappled in sunlight

Chapter 10

The Well-Educated Havanese

Puppy Kindergarten

The average Havanese is an extremely intelligent dog with a strong desire to please. All things considered he would rather do the right thing than not and gains considerable confidence by understanding what is expected of him. That understanding should begin early in life - waiting until your puppy is a totally delinquent adolescent before you start teaching him anything is simply not fair to the puppy.

In recent years, the concept of "puppy kindergarten", which provides very basic training and socialization for puppies in a friendly group setting, has caught on nearly nationwide and most communities now have these classes available. They are wonderful for Havanese, and it is well worth the effort involved to find a class near you.

Generally, in order to be enrolled in puppy kindergarten, owners need to provide proof of vaccination, and puppies should have had at least two, and preferably all three, of their puppy-shots before starting. Good places to ask about puppy kindergarten classes are your vet's office and at the nearest large chain pet store, many of which offer these classes. The training method used is almost always positive reinforcement but be sure to ask before signing up.

Home Schooling

One can also employ the services of a "personal trainer" who will come to your house and train your puppy, but unless you are actually housebound for health reasons, classes are far better for a Havanese than home-schooling as he gets to meet and interact with other puppies, which is really important for good socialization. If you do employ a private trainer, make sure that you are being trained along with your dog, or you will be wasting the trainer's time and your money.

There are many excellent dog training books on the market and, if you are a real self-starter, you can certainly attempt to train your dog and yourself simultaneously by purchasing one. The problem is - *which one?* Most new owners buy two or three books and read them all before even starting, which is a big mistake. Each writer of a dog training book is a professional dog trainer (one would hope!) and each professional dog trainer's methods are based on a slightly different underlying philosophy, some of which work for Havanese and some of which, frankly, do not. Training methods that rely entirely on food rewards, for example, (and the advocates of this method are not surprisingly referred to as "foodies" within the training world) are not likely to be successful when training a food-finicky breed like Havanese, although they work remarkably well on a breed like the Pug, who will do literally *anything* for food, or anything they think *may* be food, or even may *result* in food anytime in the near future.

The bottom line is this - if you've never trained a dog before, you are likely to end up thoroughly confused by the conflicting information you will read. The novice owner is really far better off in class, where the teacher is there to guide both you *and* your Havanese.

Beyond the Basics

Once you and your Havanese have successfully completed a training class and you are the proud owner of a well-mannered little dog, you may decide you are ready to test your talents and wish to achieve some public recognition for your efforts as a team.

The most basic recognition for a well-mannered dog is the AKC Canine Good Citizen Certificate and a dog doesn't even need to be AKC-registered to get one. Started in 1989, CGC is a program designed to reward dogs who have good manners both at home and in the community. The Canine Good Citizen Program stresses responsible pet ownership for owners and basic good manners for dogs. Dogs who pass the 10-step CGC test receive a certificate from the American Kennel Club. In addition, the Canine Good

Citizen Program lays the foundation for other AKC activities such as obedience, agility, tracking, and other performance events. Some Therapy Dog organizations also use the AKC Canine Good Citizen Test as a key component in their certification programs. Local AKC dog clubs, private trainers, and the pet "super stores" can all generally provide information on CGC testing in your area.

Requirements for an
AKC Canine Good Citizen Certificate:

Owner must sign a Responsible Dog Owners Pledge.

Accompanied by his owner (except for Item 10) and on lead, the dog must behave appropriately during the following tests:

1. Accepting a friendly stranger
2. Sitting politely for petting
3. Appearance and grooming
4. Out for a walk (walking on a loose lead)
5. Walking through a crowd
6. Sit and Down on command and Staying in place.
7. Coming when called
8. Reaction to another dog
9. Reaction to distraction
10. Supervised separation

For more information on the CGC program, contact the American Kennel Club at www.akc.org.

The tester prepares to evaluate this Havanese for CGC certification

If you are so inclined, you and your Havanese can take your interest in performance events as far as you wish. Here is a rundown of what's available:

Obedience and Rally Obedience

Competitive AKC Obedience Trials are tests in which the handler and dog demonstrate their ability to work as a team, performing a set of prescribed exercises such as heeling, sits, down-stays and recall both on and off-lead in a ring. Dogs are judged on a numerical score, with 200 being a perfect score. At the higher levels of competition, dogs must clear jumps, retrieve articles they are sent for, and perform scent discrimination exercises. Dogs may earn obedience titles beginning with Companion Dog, or CD, all the way to Obedience Trial Champion, or OTCH.

Rally-O is a recent addition to the AKC Obedience world and is less rigid in structure. It is a good beginners' sport for those Havanese and owners who are new to obedience training, but would like to try their hand at competition in a less formal setting. Spayed and neutered dogs are eligible to compete in Obedience events.

Photo by Patrick Cagney

The speedy and agile Havanese excels at performance sports.

Agility

Currently the fastest-growing sport in the world of dogs, Agility is a race against the clock. Dogs and their handlers complete an obstacle course, in which the dog has to run through a tunnel, navigate weave-poles, jump through a tire, and clear hurdles, among other things, all while a clock is running. Havanese, being both fast and agile, uniformly love Agility work and do really well at it. It is fast, exciting, and fun for both the owner and the dog, but it is also important to know that the dogs run the course with the handler running alongside, so this is *not* a sport for the sedentary! Based on their speed and accuracy in negotiating a course, dogs can earn a multitude of AKC Agility titles, or they can simply compete for fun at local events. As with Obedience, this sport also welcomes spayed and neutered dogs.

Photo by Patrick Cagney

Speed and precision are required to succeed on the agility course.

Freestyle and Flyball

Though these sports are still at the exhibition level, and no AKC titles are granted, both Freestyle, where dogs and handlers perform routines to music, and Flyball, a high-speed game where teams of dogs of various sizes retrieve over hurdles at lightning speed, are fun for owners, spectators, and dogs alike. Havanese have a lot of fun with these activities.

Dog Shows

In recent years, dog shows have gotten a lot of TV coverage, and many people wonder what they are really about. The sport of AKC Conformation, which is what dog shows represent, is second only to hunting competitions in both tradition and longevity and dates back, in this country, to the late nineteenth century when sporting men would gather to evaluate one another's breeding stock. In spite of the glamour associated with dog shows, not much has really changed from those early days.

In the AKC Conformation ring dogs and bitches are evaluated in separate classes against the standard for the breed and the dog or bitch who, in the opinion of the judge, most closely *conforms* (which is where the word *conformation* actually comes from) to the Standard on that day, wins that class. All the class winners then compete in either Winners Dog or Winners Bitch classes and the winners of those two classes are awarded points toward their AKC championship. (A dog must accrue a total of fifteen points to achieve an AKC Championship. The number of points awarded to the Winners dog and bitch at each show is based on the number of entries in his breed on that day, with five points being the maximum awarded at any show. Two of the wins a dog needs to "finish", or become an AKC Champion, must be "major" wins, which simply means they must be three points or more on the day.)

Winners Dog and Winners bitch then compete again in the Best of Breed class, which is also open to champions. The Best of Breed winner

Exhibitors ready their dogs for judging in the Best of Breed class

goes on to represent his breed in his respective group. (Havanese compete in the Toy Group.) The 7 Group winners finally compete for Best in Show, at the end of the day, and one dog is ultimately chosen Best in Show from among thousands of entries in 150 different breeds.

In addition to being a good specimen of its breed, each dog must be presented to the judge trained to gait properly and to "stack", or stand for inspection (which Toy dogs like the Havanese must do on a small table in consideration of the judges' knees!) and must be groomed in accordance with his breed's standard.

As in the early days (and *unlike* most other AKC sports) the backbone

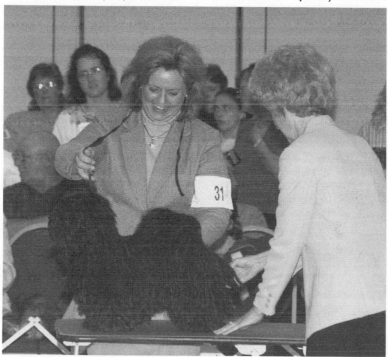

The handler stacks the Havanese on the table for the judge's examination

of this one is still comprised primarily of breeders, as this is still where they evaluate their own stock, as well as that of their friends and enemies, and measure progress made in a breed. Many breeders, for reasons of convenience, hire professional handlers to show their dogs, and just as many probably show their own.

Anyone can compete with their dog in a dog show, however, provided the dog is AKC registered and not spayed or neutered - which is logical in a sport whose underlying purpose is the evaluation of breeding animals. Indeed, many talented amateur owners have competed successfully against the professionals over the years, and many make a family sport of it, with involvement in Junior Showmanship for the younger family members. This is not a sport for the faint-hearted, though, as competition is remarkably fierce for a venue in which all you generally win are points toward a championship and a few colored ribbons...and it still takes a good dog to win!

Therapy Dogs

One of the most rewarding things you and your Havanese can do is to become involved in therapy work. Although not a sport, per se, surely there is no more worthwhile way to spend time with your friend than in brightening the lives of those less fortunate.

Therapy dogs are used in nursing homes, hospitals, and other facilities

Therapy dogs usually wear some identifying item, such as this cape, when visiting facilities.

The other side of this cape says, "Ask to pet me, I'm friendly."

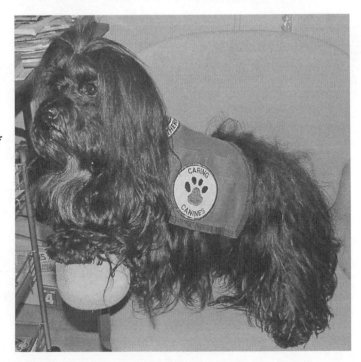

where the occupants may not be able to visit with dogs on a regular basis, and their presence is generally welcomed by both patients and staff.

Havanese are especially suited to this work for several reasons. Their small size makes them both easily portable and non-threatening, their odorless coats are generally non-irritating even to those with allergies, and their remarkably intuitive nature makes them very good at the job, which they seem to understand instinctively. They can provide quiet comfort when needed, or they can be charming and funny when someone needs cheering, or they can sit patiently on the lap of a child in the Read To Rover program, listening carefully and sympathetically as the child struggles to read aloud.

Photo by Donna Henley

This therapy dog relaxes and listens to a story during a Read to Rover visit

There are several national Therapy Dog organizations, which certify therapy dogs, and many communities have groups that organize activities on a local level. If you are of a non-competitive (or non-physical) nature, yet would still like to get out and do something with your Havanese, certifying him to become a therapy dog might just be perfect for both of you.

Pet Action Shots

Beautiful, intelligent, versatile and lovable...this is

The Havanese